ISO 9000 FOR EXECUTIVES

Dr. Jack E. Small

ISO 9000 FOR EXECUTIVES

Understand the Fastest Growing Program to Impact American Industry and Commerce

Dr. Jack E. Small

Lanchester Press Inc.
P. O. Box 60621
Sunnyvale, CA 94086

Lanchester Press Inc. P.O. Box 60621, Sunnyvale CA 94086
© 1995 by Dr. Jack E. Small
Published   1995
Printed in the United States of America by Patson's
Press, Inc. Sunnyvale CA 94086

Library of Congress Catalog Card Number: 95-77627

ISBN: 1-57321-001-3

Lanchester Press Inc.
P. O. Box 60621
Sunnyvale, CA 94086

Thanks to Marilyn, my wife and best friend, for her love, support and understanding and to Jennifer, my wonderful daughter, who makes me very proud.

Contents

Illustrations

1 INTRODUCTION

In today's highly competitive business environment, there is little debate on the merits of quality and what the pursuit of better or improved quality can mean to a company's future. However, at the workers' level, quality remains an abstract concept that relies on a religious-like belief or faith that following prescribed procedures will result in the attainment of success. The inherent aspects of many quality programs ask one to accept their pronouncements and somehow, magically, the desired results will be achieved. Of course, this is never a one-time thing; one must constantly keep the vigil and continually practice the good things, or else the program will fail.

In attempting to implement various quality programs, we often see the practitioners questioning the value of the approach or doubting the cause and effect relationship. Many times, those who are asked to implement these quality plans will say, "Yes, but what can I do?" or "What difference will my contribution make?" This inability to link the day-to-day work activities with the lofty quality ideals has caused many quality programs to fail in the past.

Many of the current problems associated with quality and its implementation in the work force stem from the reliance on belief or faith without drawing the direct relationship to workers' roles and responsibilities. People have to see how a focus on their daily work activities (and subsequent improvement of these functions) can make a difference.

The advent of ISO 9000 has brought a practicality to quality and, in essence, a "do" function has arrived. Individuals can now participate by concentrating on what they do, when they do it, how they do it, why they do it, etc. Through these basic actions, they can get a feel and understanding for their respective contributions to the whole. Workers begin to see how their efforts (or lack thereof) can make a marked difference. The net result is that people now can see how their actions will have a direct result on an organization's overall quality results.

In addition, ISO 9000 provides a foundation for a total quality management program by concentrating on three fundamental aspects: 1) implementing quality controls, 2) documenting the various processes and procedures so there is no misunderstanding or miscommunication, and 3) ensuring that the appropriate quality emphasis is established and followed by everyone in the organization. Admittedly, these acts result in a minimum level of quality achievement, but they do produce essential levels of consistency and repeatability.

There are several major reasons for incorporating the use of the ISO 9000 international quality standards within the scope of your company's quality efforts, but absolutely first and foremost is that YOUR CUSTOMERS WANT IT!

International customers have started to make ISO 9000 compliance an integral part of their purchase agreements. Even those customers who have not adopted this requirement are beginning to use the standards as a way to differentiate the offerings of various suppliers; particularly when products and services are substantially similar. In spite of the fact that ISO 9000 is not a total quality management approach, customers (both private sector as well as government purchasing organizations) see compliance as a way to gain a degree of assurance that suppliers are "doing what they say they are doing."

Competitive pressures are also beginning to emerge as motivators in seeking ISO 9000 compliance. Many companies have converted their ISO 9000 successes into a marketing advantage and have used this achievement as a fundamental advertising strategy, aimed at separating one vendor from the rest by virtue of the ISO 9000 registration. ISO 9000 alone is not indicative of a good quality company; however, substantial evidence suggests that it does represent a documented foundation that will complement additional quality initiatives. To the extent that ISO 9000 is better understood and more widely adopted, it will certainly provide a competitive advantage for all companies that will be vying in today's fast-paced, highly-competitive global economy!

Most compliant companies have realized a substantial degree of employee enthusiasm for the ISO 9000 program. Part of this has to do with the fact that the employees are empowered. By asking them to document the realities of their jobs, the results often reflect conditions of "what should be" rather than the "what is" or "what was."

By taking the time to analyze and document the various processes, gaps have been closed, illogical flaws identified and corrected, and numerous redundancies eliminated. Completing the preparation for an ISO 9000 registration provides a basis for understanding where and how a person fits into the total equation. It becomes readily apparent how one individual can make a difference and how their respective contribution can influence the results of the total entity. Many of the abstract elements of quality are reduced to fundamental tasks and have become more understandable to the "do-er."

ISO 9000 is one of the truly remarkable quality programs to arrive on the international business scene. It is not difficult to understand; it has proven to be valuable and not a time-waster. Most importantly, ISO 9000 is for EVERYONE! Fundamentally, ISO 9000 will affect your bottom line. It will provide a FRAMEWORK FOR CONTROL—by enabling both the intra-and inter-communications throughout your organization and allowing you to get a handle on the troublesome operational aspects of your business. ISO 9000, in a nutshell, is COMMON SENSE! (Figure 1.1)

One of the most remarkable aspects of ISO 9000 is that these quality standards are not designed to improve the quality of the supplier or provider of a service! Although there clearly is an emphasis on the key elements of one's business, the underlying philosophy is not truly aimed at making you better. In actuality, the standards are designed to give assurance to your clients or customers that you are "doing what you say you are doing." In today's highly competitive business environment, companies will attempt to attract customers by citing their quality achievements and stating that their visions and objectives are world class, the best, the acknowledged leader in their field, the superlative quality provider, etc. But, how are customers and potential customers to know which of these companies is actually achieving its quality goals? Or, put another way, which of these companies is not only "talking the talk" but "walking the walk"—in effect, "doing what they say they are doing?"

ISO 9000 is the vehicle that will allow companies or organizations to prove they are doing what their pronouncements say they are doing. Demonstrating conformance to the ISO 9000 standards will provide the opportunity to unequivocally state one's quality objectives (through documentation of the key operational procedures), ensure that all of these procedures are being followed throughout the organization, and prove that the objectives are being accomplished (proved to not only the company's personnel, but to the outside world).

As with other quality assessment programs, the ISO 9000 standard has both positive and negative aspects. Some have argued that the standard itself is too low; there is practically no emphasis on customer satisfaction; its language is too ambiguous; it emphasizes documentation over true quality methods and metrics and there is no value differentiation, since results are not evaluated. The circumstances surrounding registration can be vague and confusing, particularly for U.S. firms marketing products and services abroad.

ISO 9000

FIGURE 1.1

Understanding customer requirements is, however, one of the keys to quality. A company left in the dark about the need for an emphasis on quality is probably in the dark about other matters, too. Conversely, a company that understands whether or not a customer expects ISO 9000 registration may well be on the way toward building a sound quality system. The ISO 9000 standards are a template for the creation of such a program, regardless of whether or not the target market is in the U.S. or overseas. By embarking on an ISO 9000 journey, one can expect lower costs, improved customer satisfaction, greater brand loyalty, and stronger market performance associated with this quality effort. The ISO 9000 quality process will prove to be an important step on the road to Total Quality Management and will ultimately provide real and substantial value to your shareholders.

2 BACKGROUND AND EVOLUTION OF ISO 9000

In 1987, the International Organization for Standardization (a Geneva-based, 100-member-nation organization—see Appendix 1) adopted a set of quality standards known as ISO 9000. These standards attempted to consolidate the proliferation of quality terms, harmonize the various individual country quality requirements and deal with the approaching unification of the European market by presenting a single, agreed-to set of quality standards for use by international suppliers of goods and services. (It should be noted that the prefix "ISO" in ISO 9000 is not the abbreviation for the International Organization for Standardization, but actually comes from the Greek and is pronounced "eye-so" and means "equal"...as in "ISO-BAR," "ISOTHERM" or "ISOCELES TRIANGLE").

Thus, the ISO 9000 quality standards mean the same for any organization or company doing business, regardless of the country where the entity demonstrates conformity. By adopting the ISO 9000 quality series as an international standard, the emphasis is on a worldwide basis and implies assurance that the ISO 9000 registration will mean the same thing, wherever in the world one does business.

During the latter part of the 1970's, the International Organization for Standardization established a Technical Committee (TC#176) which began working on the creation of the ISO 9000 quality series. The Technical Committee published a white paper entitled, "Vision 2000 - the Strategy for International Standards Implementation in the Quality Arena During the 1990's." In essence, this white paper provides a road map for the how's and why's of quality by the year 2000.

The ground rules for the standards outlined four self-explanatory goals:

1. UNIVERSAL ACCEPTANCE
2. CURRENT COMPATIBILITY
3. FORWARD COMPATIBILITY
4. FORWARD FLEXIBILITY

However, the most important aspect contained in Vision 2000 was the fact that the quality standards were NOT aimed at specific products or industries; but were in fact, GENERIC in nature. The idea was to create a set of standards that could be applied to any company or organization, regardless of the specific output or nature of the business. Thus, the ISO 9000 standards were established to apply to a company doing business in some or all of these categories:

A) HARDWARE—producing any and all products which consist of manufactured pieces, parts and/or their respective assemblies—anything from anvils to zippers. If you're a supplier of a tangible, hardware product, the ISO 9000 standards will apply to you.

B) SOFTWARE—an acknowledgment of the Information Technology or Data Processing community. Here, the generic category encompasses a variety of products such as computer software as well as any other type of recorded information including concepts, transactions or procedures. Again, if you are a supplier or provider of these types of tangible products, ISO 9000 applies to you.

C) PROCESSED MATERIALS This category includes products (both final and intermediate) which consist of solids, liquids, gasses, and their various combinations. It also includes a variety of other materials such as filaments or sheet structures, ingots, and other processed materials that are typically delivered in containers, drums, bags, tanks, cans, pipelines, rolls, etc. If your business involves this area, ISO 9000 will apply.

D) SERVICES The most all-encompassing of the four generic categories. This area deals with the intangible entities which may be the entire or main offering, but also includes activities such as selling, consulting, delivering, training, improving, evaluating, operating, or servicing for a tangible and/or a non-tangible product. One way to visualize the scope of this area is to think of services as a continuum. At one end is a provider of service for a tangible product (such as an auto repair mechanic who services a tangible product —your car). The mid-range of this continuum would be a waiter/waitress (they do not design the food, create it, — package it, or price it... but they bring it to your table - i.e., deliver it). At the far end of this continuum would be a provider of service for intangible products, e.g., advice or intellectual information such as one would receive from an accountant, an educator, an analyst, a consultant, a physician, an attorney, etc. If your particular business falls anywhere on this continuum, then ISO 9000 would apply to you (Figure 2.1).

It becomes readily apparent that ISO 9000 applies to EVERYONE! It's not just for manufacturers, transportation companies, electronic and computer manufacturers, or those in the chemical industry, but for anyone providing a good or service who needs to assure

SERVICES

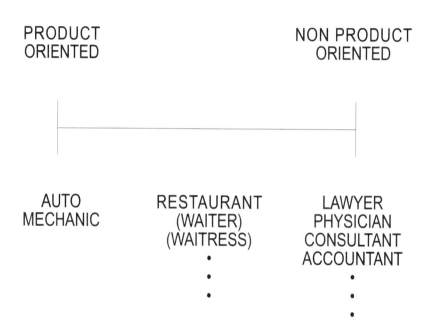

PRODUCT
ORIENTED

NON PRODUCT
ORIENTED

AUTO
MECHANIC

RESTAURANT
(WAITER)
(WAITRESS)
•
•
•

LAWYER
PHYSICIAN
CONSULTANT
ACCOUNTANT
•
•
•

FIGURE 2.1

customers that they are doing what they say they are doing in terms of quality. Combined with its simplicity and usefulness, ISO 9000 represents a quality approach for virtually every known business.

Following the publication of Vision 2000, TC #176 produced the set of international quality standards (known as ISO 9000) which were designed for "Quality Assurance Management Systems." Their purpose is to assure that a quality system is in place and is being followed. For companies demonstrating compliance with the ISO 9000 standards, the results will be the delivery of products and services in a CONSISTENT and REPEATABLE manner. Demonstration of compliance with the standards requires an on-site audit of the quality system by an impartial, "accredited" auditor. This auditor will verify that the quality system complies with the ISO 9000 standard and that everyone involved is following the documented procedures.

In essence, ISO 9000 involves three basic actions: (1) establishing the proper quality management controls, (2) documenting those controls (developing a Quality Manual) which creates a detailed record of an organization's quality procedures and (3) making sure that everyone in the organization or group follows the established practices (Figure 2.2).

Fundamentally, ISO 9000 can be summarized as:

1. SAY WHAT YOU DO   establish appropriate quality controls and systems
2. DO WHAT YOU SAY   ensure that everyone involved follows the established processes
3. SHOW ME   demonstrate compliance of your quality system to an external auditor

The ISO 9000 focus is directed both internally at an organization's processes and methods and externally at controlling and assuring the quality of products and/or services being provided or shipped. ISO 9000 does not deal with the whole of an organization's or company's quality system, and it tends to emphasize the purchaser's requirements rather than the producer's. Generally, the need for standards in business transactions arises on the purchaser's side, and this has

KEYS

- ESTABLISH CONTROLS
- ENSURE EVERYONE COMPLIES
- DOCUMENT PROCESSES

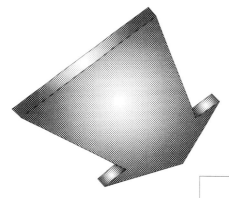

SAY WHAT YOU DO!

DO WHAT YOU SAY!

SHOW ME!

FIGURE 2.2

often led to standards development oriented with the purchaser in mind. It is the purchaser who bears the burden of direct loss due to poor quality, and it is the purchaser who is concerned with the need to buy the right product. One way to address these concerns is through the establishment of appropriate quality standards.

The ISO 9000 quality standards are designed to address these concerns. The requirements are organized in a logical manner, and establishing quality management in accordance with the standards is an effective way of starting to build a quality system. The use of these standards can also enable companies to improve their existing quality systems.

Certainly, there are other standards and standardized approaches to quality, e.g., the U.S. DOD Standard, and the Malcolm Baldrige Award criteria in the United States. None of these, however, attempt to put quality on a global footing. To this end, ISO 9000 is written for use by the widest possible audience. As a result, the ISO 9000 series offers suggestions rather than issuing specific, prescriptive solutions. It does not explicitly dictate which quality management system to use, but offers requirements that the supplier's quality system should address.

Historically, the ISO 9000 standards were created from a chain of earlier military and governmental quality standards, i.e., U.S. military (Mil-Q-9858A), NATO (AQAP-1), Great Britain (Def Stan 05-21) and United States (10 CFR 50). In 1979, the British Standards Institution issued "BS 5750," which, along with the other existing standards such as the Canadian "Z-299" quality standards, became the eventual basis for the present ISO 9000 international standards (Figure 2.3). After ISO 9000 was issued, the British Standards Institution revised "BS 5750" to conform to the new composite standard.

Since adoption of the ISO 9000 series of standards is left to each country individually, one of the modifications a country will make is to translate the international standards into their own language (and in doing so, change the titles, i.e., ISO 9000 is called "AS 3900" in Australia, "BNS180" in Barbados, and "Q9000" in the United

States—see Appendix 3). Although the standards may have different names, by virtue of the fact that these are international standards, the content and structure are the same.

One of the key aspects of ISO 9000 is that the quality standards do NOT apply to specific products. The standards are generic in nature and are intended to enable a supplier (through a combination of internal and external audits) to provide assurance that there is a quality system in place, it is fully deployed, and this quality system will allow the supplier to meet the stated quality objectives.

In actuality, the "what" that is produced (the end product or service) is essentially immaterial to the ISO 9000 registration process. An ISO 9000 registration is, in effect, a confirmation of the processes only! It is for this reason that the registration to the ISO 9000 standards is never indicated on the products themselves, but can only appear on the product literature or advertising.

The ISO 9000 standards were originally developed for use in contractual situations (such as those that exist between a supplier and a customer). There are provisions within the application of the standard for self-audits ("first-party") and, of course, the customer ("second-party") can request an audit of the operation as a condition of doing business. There are a number of quality systems operated as "second-party" programs, such as the U.S. Food and Drug Administration (for medical device manufacturers) and the Department of Defense.

However, the ISO 9000 program goes beyond this customer audit requirement by establishing the need for an independent, impartial auditor — commonly referred to as the "third-party" assessor or the "registrar." Through the use of these objective auditors who have, themselves, complied with the specifics found in the ISO 10000 series of standards (which deal with the behavior, training, performance, ethics, etc. of auditors), customers can be assured that the ISO 9000 registration of a company or supplier has been performed in a standardized, agreed-to manner. In addition to the actual Registration Assessment, these third-party, external auditors will continue to audit a company on a regularly scheduled basis (approximately every six months). These surveillance audits are not surprise visits, but are

HISTORY

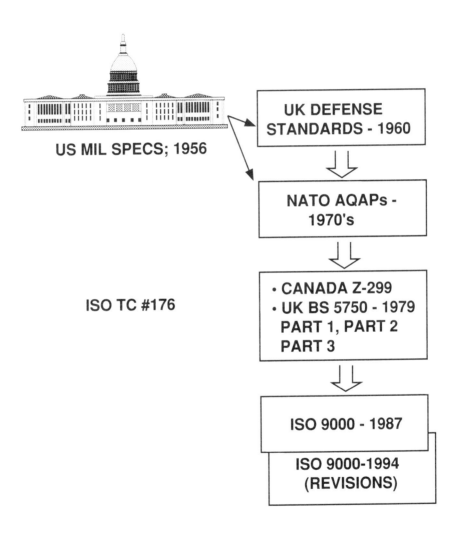

FIGURE 2.3

established and scheduled to ensure that a company maintains its quality focus as the organization dynamically changes over time. Most ISO 9000 registrations are in effect for a two-or three-year period (depending on the registration firm employed). When the registration has expired, the entire quality system is re-evaluated, and the cycle continues. There is no end point in this process —it is forever!

Unfortunately, some of the clauses of ISO 9000 tend to be overly dogmatic and, in several cases, require some actions and details that many suppliers have ignored or omitted over time. One must keep in mind that the underlying principles of ISO 9000 are established for the benefit of the purchaser or customer and, therefore, may not always be in the best interests of the supplier.

In spite of this bureaucracy, adhering to the specifics of the ISO 9000 standards will demonstrate to your customers that you are willing to listen to what they want and respond accordingly. If one truly seeks to not only satisfy but delight one's customers, and if the customers are asking for ISO 9000 compliance, then it only makes sense to accommodate their needs within the best of your abilities.

3 OVERVIEW
(ISO 9000 - What it is and What it is Not!)

What is the real story behind ISO 9000? Is it really a bureaucratic nightmare running amuck? Are the benefits merely a smoke screen? Are unscrupulous charlatans offering consulting guidance and naive and untrained auditors sucking corporate monies for unnecessary services? Most of these arguments have been swirling around ISO 9000 since it first appeared in 1987. Part of the reason for these concerns is the huge amount of misunderstanding and misconception regarding the program.

ISO 9000 is fairly simple to understand. It is not complex, nor is it difficult to comprehend. Most of the difficulties with ISO 9000 lie in its implementation efforts and the subsequent translation from a generic set of quality guidelines to the specifics of a given company's operations. The fact is that ISO 9000 does not prescribe a uniform quality system, but allows a wide variety of quality implementations based on the needs of an organization's projects, products or services.

Perhaps the best way to view ISO 9000 is by analyzing its major components and recognizing its underlying philosophy. Once you realize where ISO 9000 is aimed, it is relatively easy to see why and how it can help your company in its quality efforts.

ISO 9000 is a series of international quality standards designed for quality assurance management systems. The requirements are aimed at achieving customer satisfaction by creating an environment for CONSISTENCY and REPEATABILITY in all relevant stages of a company's operation. Fundamentally, ISO 9000 provides focus in two ways:

1. Ensuring that your company has established appropriate quality POLICIES and PRACTICES in your operations, and

2. Ensuring that the above POLICIES and PRACTICES are being followed by everyone.

ISO 9000 provides the framework for ensuring that your company performs a variety of things which will address quality. Most importantly, it verifies that everyone in your organization actually does what they say they are doing! By concentrating on these fundamental aspects, a company is asked to state its quality objectives and MAKE SURE that whatever is being stated is, indeed, what the company is doing! That's it— no more, no less. In essence, a company says, "This is what we do to ensure quality, and everyone in our organization is, in fact, doing it." Now, that type of statement is fairly straightforward and simple, but as noted earlier, the ability to actually perform up to the stated objectives and to be able to prove performance is the crux of the difficulty.

ISO 9000 does not attempt to define what makes good quality, nor does it act as a cookbook by outlining the exact steps an organization should follow to guarantee quality. It simply identifies the various elements that should be addressed by ANY business (hardware, software, processed materials or services), regardless of the specific nature of its operations. It notes the type of questions a common-sense individual would ask and challenges the prospective applicant to show how, why, and when certain quality-assurance measures are taken.

The first fundamental aspect of ISO 9000 is that it focuses solely on PROCESSES and not PRODUCTS (Figure 3.1). In fact, it never looks at the end product or result of your operations. ISO 9000 concentrates on the various processes an organization will utilize to bring its goods or services to the marketplace. The heart of ISO 9000 is that it looks to see that you have appropriate practices established (and that these are not hollow statements, but you are actually following these steps). Many ISO 9000-compliant companies will incorrectly identify one of their products as being "ISO 9000." This is absolutely false. The end result is never judged, therefore, it would be wrong to indicate that the resulting good or service was somehow the recipient of an ISO 9000 acknowledgment.

Secondly, the original version of the ISO 9000 standard (1987) required a contractual relationship, which meant ISO 9000 became a condition of doing business. ISO 9000 was a way for a customer to see if a supplier conformed to some level of quality by requiring compliance with the standard as part of the contractual arrangements. Thus, ISO 9000 is fundamentally different from most of the other types of quality programs which tend to be awards or acknowledgments of a company's achievements in quality. ISO 9000 is the basic form of doing "what your customer wants." By requiring adherence to the ISO 9000 standards, a customer is stating an obvious need, "I would like some assurance that you, the supplier of a good or service, are actually doing what you say you are doing. I would also like some assurance that these measures have something to do with quality. And if I, as the customer, can receive this assurance, THEN I WILL DO BUSINESS WITH YOU."

The 1994 version of the ISO 9000 standards removed the "two party contractual purposes" aspect and replaced the concept with the notion that ISO 9000 was to be used to show that a supplier's various quality processes needed to be demonstrated. Although the explicit reference to a contractual situation is no longer there, the

IS

IS NOT

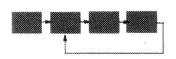

PROCESS

PRODUCT

BUSINESS CONDITION

AWARD

CUSTOMER/CLIENT

SUPPLIER

FIGURE 3.1

IS

WHAT'S

CREATIVE/
INTERPRETIVE

THIS VERIFIES THAT
YOU ACTUALLY DO
"WHAT YOU SAY YOU
ARE DOING"

IS NOT

HOW'S

PRESCRIPTIVE/
MANDATORY

THIS VERIFIES
THAT YOU HAVE
"ATTAINED QUALITY
RESULTS"

FIGURE 3.1

fact that a prospective ISO 9000 applicant must demonstrate adherence to the quality standards illustrates the point that proof is still an inherent aspect.

When one examines the essence of ISO 9000, the philosophy indicates that, contrary to popular belief, ISO 9000 does not necessarily ensure that the supplier of the goods or services will perform at a higher quality level. ISO 9000 does not necessarily make your company better, BUT what it does do is give ASSURANCE to your customers that you are doing what you say you are doing. It gives your customers the feeling that you, as a company, can stand behind your words and demonstrate that your actions are consistent with your intentions.

Thirdly, ISO 9000 is generic and applicable to ANY type of business and ANY size of business. By defining ISO 9000 in generic terms, with a focus on processes, the program can be used in an almost limitless variety of applications. It really doesn't matter what type of business you are in, whether you make products, deliver goods, or provide a type of service, you will be able to demonstrate your adherence to the ISO 9000 standards. Naturally, the way in which your particular business chooses to address the various elements of ISO 9000 will vary according to the specifics of your industry, and that is the beauty of ISO 9000. It doesn't PRESCRIBE the way to show quality, but merely provides the forum for showing your own unique ways of addressing the relevant areas. As long as you practice what you preach, you will be able to demonstrate ISO 9000 adherence.

Size of the organization is also immaterial with respect to compliance with the standards. For example, in a large, multinational corporation, the smallest group to receive an ISO 9000 certificate consisted of only nine people, while the largest group was a manufacturing and development plant in excess of 8,800 people. Regardless of their size, both were able to demonstrate that they "did what they said they did" and both achieved ISO 9000 compliance and thus received ISO 9000 certificates. You might ask why a nine-person organization decided to seek ISO 9000 registration? Simple, their customers asked them for compliance and made it a condition of doing business. The same could be said for the 8,800-person organization, although they clearly had many more complex processes than the nine-person group. The relative size and complexity of the groups did not matter. What was critical was the ability to define their own processes and be in a position to show that they were following them.

The fourth significant aspect of ISO 9000 is that the standards tell you "WHAT" is needed, but do not tell you "HOW" to accomplish the requirements. The standards, being generic, are open to creativity and interpretation, but are neither prescriptive in design nor authoritative rules for quality. By illustrating the "WHAT's" for quality, ISO 9000 can enable a company to select its own methods for demonstrating proof.

The fifth, and perhaps the most important, aspect of ISO 9000 deals with the ability to prove that your company is doing what it says it is doing. Proof is the operative word. How do you show your customers (as well as yourselves) that you have quality processes in place and you are, indeed, following these procedures? ISO 9000 uses a unique and fascinating way to demonstrate this proof. It requires an assessment by a "third-party" auditor to prove that you have established processes and are following them. (An ISO 9000 applicant is the "party of the first part" and your customers are the "parties of the second part." A "third party"is someone outside the contractual arrangement existing between the supplier of goods/services and their customers—in essence, an impartial, unbiased observer who can verify that the supplier is doing what they say they are doing). The third party does not have a vested interest in the business relationship and doesn't care whether or not the ISO 9000 registration is successful.

The auditors remain impartial to the vagaries of the business arrangement; their sole task is to ensure that the ISO 9000 applicant has taken the time to create and establish the appropriate quality processes and is following these processes throughout the organization. These third parties are commonly called "assessors" or "registrars." They perform audits of a supplier's quality system and assess whether the supplier meets the specifications as outlined in the ISO 9000 standards. Following a successful ISO 9000 audit, the auditors or registrars note, or register, a company as being compliant with the standards (hence their name). (See Chapter 8, "Registrars and Consultants")

The registrars get paid for their services and, although the expenses can be considerable, it's best to realize who will be paying for these services in the end. That's correct, the customer! But this is alright, since the customer is the one benefitting from the program. It is the customer who is receiving assurance that an ISO 9000 compliant company is doing what they say and the registrar is verifying this (on the customer's behalf).

One of the other insidious aspects to ISO 9000 is that successful registration is not a one-time process. The ISO 9000 effort is not like other "apply - perform - reward" type programs. It has continuity. For example, assume that your company establishes its quality-oriented processes; makes sure that these processes are fully deployed throughout the organization; keeps sufficient records to demonstrate this involvement; and eventually passes the final audit. This is a significant achievement, and you may take a deep bow, extend congratulations to one and all and have a party. But, you are not finished! A registrar will periodically assess your company for compliance (on a regularly scheduled program of visits— FOREVER!) These periodic visits are known as "Surveillance Audits" and they are established to make sure that a company in today's business environment, subjected to the pressures of change, continues to keep its quality focus and accommodates the changes in a way that is compliant with the philosophy and intent of the ISO 9000 standards.

Embarking on an ISO 9000 program will enable a company to ensure that it has established a necessary and sufficient set of quality processes and procedures, thoroughly document these procedures in order to allow everyone in the organization to see and understand them, and provide enough evidence that everyone is following these "established" procedures in their daily operations. The net result will be a set of quality-oriented processes that are CONSISTENT and REPEATABLE. These processes, when implemented, will start your company on the road to becoming a better quality organization. (Figure 3.2) Another way to look at ISO 9000 is to review the statements found in Figure 3.3, which outline the ten quality commandments of an ISO 9000 program. They will serve as your guide for the rest of this book.

In spite of the overwhelming support being given to the ISO 9000 efforts, another set of arguments continue to be promulgated which point out the many faults with the current set of standards. To illustrate the arguments, the following excerpts are from a mythical debate between Mr. A. Gainst and Mr. I.M. Fore (both leading quality experts):

A. Gainst: "I don't have a problem with the basic principles of ISO 9000, but I really object to the pressure being placed on companies to meet these requirements. Not all companies are in a position to support this commitment, given the tough economic times...."

I.M. Fore: "In many cases, the pressure is self imposed... since the standards truly represent a "common sense" approach they deal with those things that any business should have been doing all along. Although many companies reacted to the EC (European Community) '91 directive, it appears that the private sector customers are now driving the effort and the pressure is a reaction to customer demands — in much the same way as the demand for new functions or new price levels. To use the tough economic times argument is specious, there will always be a reason not to do something. Or, put another way, do you really want to continue doing things poorly in the name of economy?"

A. Gainst: "Well, I should point out that companies do not need to be ISO 9000 registered to subscribe to the principles of good quality procedures. In today's world it's no longer acceptable for businesses to ship poor qual-

CONSISTENCY & REPEATABILITY

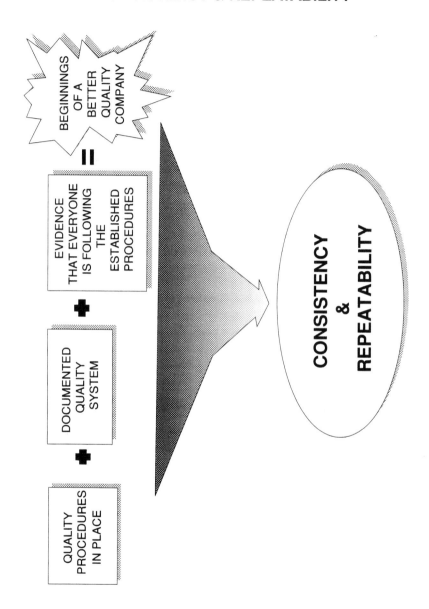

FIGURE 3.2

ity goods, and the standards should be regarded as unwritten policies and procedures by which companies should operate."

I.M. Fore: "I agree that's how companies should operate... but the real question is how do the customers or purchasers know that the companies are in fact operating with the proper principles in effect (the old ISO 9000 bywords of 'saying what you do and doing what you say')."

A. Gainst: "Most successful companies are probably following many of the ISO 9000 guidelines anyway, whether they realize it or not. The receipt of an ISO 9000 registration is nothing more than a piece of paper — it doesn't guarantee anything."

I.M. Fore: "Companies that are already practicing good quality procedures/practices don't have a problem with compliance. In fact, in most cases, the seeking of ISO 9000 actually helped improve the overall operations (by focusing attention on those details which may have slipped by).

As for the guarantee, I agree. All it says is that a company took the time to implement the controls, document those areas and, most importantly, demonstrate that they are following these common -sense concepts. At a minimum, it guarantees that the processes will be consistent, uniformly followed and repeatable."

A. Gainst: "I'm glad you mentioned minimum because that is exactly what ISO 9000 represents, a minimum approach to quality. It certainly isn't a total quality management approach."

QUALITY
COMMANDMENTS

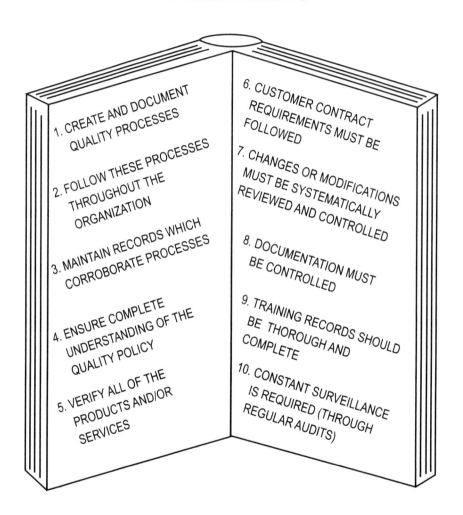

FIGURE 3.3

I.M. Fore: "Well at least we agree on that...ISO 9000 is at best a first step and should be regarded that way...but it is a good start."

A. Gainst: "One of the biggest hoaxes brought out in the name of quality has been the "need to seek ISO 9000 because it is REQUIRED in order to business in Europe." Did you know no "LAW" requires ISO 9000 compliance for products to be sold in Europe?"

I.M. Fore: "Again we seem to be in agreement. You're correct in stating there is no "LAW." The EC created a series of "Directives" (for their member countries) but never, in fact, made it law. However, what we are seeing are literally thousands of customer requests (both in the private sector as well as country governmental agencies) requiring ISO 9000 as a condition of doing business. At this point in time, a "Law" is probably not necessary!"

A. Gainst: "Yes, many customers are asking for ISO 9000 but that is because they think ISO 9000 is the cure-all for all their quality ills... and it simply is not!"

I.M. Fore: "ISO 9000 is the starting point for quality... NOT THE END GOAL. By asking companies to demonstrate their commitment to quality principles and to be willing to stand behind their word, customers see an ISO 9000 registration as one way to obtain a degree of assurance that a company is worth doing business with. ISO 9000 is not a panacea of quality, but merely one step along the way."

A.Gainst: "But at what price? ISO 9000 is a regulatory nightmare. The long-term effects may be negligible. And
what about the costs? How can we survive with registration costs, consulting costs, education, manuals, assessments, and all the other associated expenses of seeking an ISO 9000 registration growing at an astronomi-
cal rate?"

I.M. Fore: "Many of the costs are containable and some can be
reduced or eliminated through good business practices. Studies have shown that the bulk of the costs
associated with ISO 9000 are internal—that is the
costs of establishing controls and ensuring that these
controls reflect the way things are being done. By analyzing the various procedures, we have uncovered numerous instances of duplication of effort, gaps or holes
in the processes and waste and inefficiencies. It's true
that ISO 9000 is not free— what is? But most companies have found they will recover their costs in anywhere from one to three years due to greater productivity or elimination of wasteful and costly operations.
The return on investment is there; one only needs to
take advantage of it."

........on and on it goes........ .

To summarize, the following set of typical questions and answers will help illustrate the significance of an ISO 9000 program:

1. DO THE ISO 9000 STANDARDS REQUIRE COMPLIANCE OF MY PROCESSES OR, IN SOME SPECIFIC INSTANCES, ARE MY PRODUCTS REQUIRED TO BECOME CERTIFIED OR REGISTERED?

   The ISO 9000 standards do NOT apply to specific products. The standards are generic in nature and are intended to enable a company, through a combination of internal and external audits, to provide assurance that it has a quality system in place. The quality system will, in turn, allow the company to meet its stated quality objectives.

   In actuality, "what" is produced is immaterial to the audit process. The ISO 9000 registration is a confirmation of the processes only! It is for this reason that registration to the ISO 9000 standards is never indicated on the products themselves, but can only appear on the product literature or in the company advertising.

2. DOES ISO 9000 GUARANTEE A LEVEL OF QUALITY FOR MY FINISHED PRODUCT OR THE SERVICE I PROVIDE?

   Everyone who has gone through a basic course on ISO 9000 knows this to be patently untrue. A successful registration will allow for CONSISTENCY and REPEATABILITY; but given the current level of the standards, there is no value assessment. The old adage of "garbage in - garbage out" unfortunately holds, but with the added modifier that the resulting garbage will be consistent and repeatable.

3. WILL I HAVE AN ESTABLISHED QUALITY SYSTEM IN PLACE IF I SUCCESSFULLY PASS MY REGISTRATION AUDIT?

Passing an ISO 9000 final assessment is just the beginning, and the reality is that a quality system (and all that it implies) doesn't really begin to take hold until after all the employees assimilate the task of maintaining the documentation. It generally will take at least two surveillance audits before the documentation is mature.

ISO 9000 is, in essence, the first step toward total quality management... or the foundation upon which to build a functioning quality program. It is by no means the FINAL STAGE! Remember, your customers define their quality expectations, and the ISO 9000 compliance is but one link in a long chain of events which ultimately lead to customer satisfaction. What ISO 9000 delivers is an external confirmation to your customers that a quality system is in place and is being followed!

4. IS THE ISO 9000 REGISTRATION CERTIFICATE A PRIZE OR AN AWARD GRANTED BY THE INTERNATIONAL ORGANIZATION FOR STANDARDIZATION?

ISO 9000 is not an award (like the Malcolm Baldrige Award or other similar awards). The key should be to understand the standard, incorporate the methodology within a company's quality system, and utilize the spirit to move forward.

5. IS ISO 9000 A "PRESCRIPTIVE WAY" TO ESTABLISH GOOD QUALITY PROCEDURES... ESPECIALLY IN A COMPANY SEEKING TO EMBARK ON THE ROAD TO GOOD QUALITY?

ISO 9000 is NOT intended to be prescriptive in any way, shape, or form. In fact, any attempt to make the standards prescriptive in nature has been consistently voted down. The generic approach of ISO 9000 has given it the flexibility to be adaptive to any and all quality approaches. This latitude allows registrants to seek their own quality levels and establish the proper quality system that is right for their own particular organization.

6. I HAVE HEARD THAT ISO 9000 STIFLES FLEXIBILITY, CREATES UNNECESSARY WORK AND ERECTS BARRICADES TO CHANGE... IS THIS TRUE?

Much of this criticism comes from the fact that most companies have a tendency to over-document their procedures and go overboard in their desire to present as complete a system as possible.

The resultant documentation monster is a self-created one, and often companies must learn this the hard way by trying to live with the system they've created. Too much documentation makes it difficult, if not impossible, to do everything that has been written down.

This learning takes place during the audits, and one way out of the trap is to re-focus and re-analyze your quality program. Generally, the procedures will become simpler and less error-prone (sometimes they even become more user-friendly).

7. DOES ISO 9000 CREATE A MONOLITHIC ROUTINE THAT IS HEAVILY STRUCTURED AND OPPOSED TO CHANGE?

If the documentation is improper, this may occur. One of the key elements is to allow the system to accommodate change and retain its flexibility in the face of seemingly rigid consistency.

ISO 9000 only provides the framework for creating procedures. A company seeking to establish processes must be very careful to remain creative and not let the procedures become onerous to the point that they stifle creativity.

8. HOW CAN ISO 9000 PROFESS TO ADDRESS QUALITY WHEN IT IS MISSING THE ELEMENT OF "CONTINUOUS IMPROVEMENT?"

While ISO 9000 does not explicitly require continuous improvement, (a frequent criticism of the program), the combination of the ever-present management review, the extensive internal audits and the essential corrective action clauses tend to result in an improvement cycle process (one that is ALWAYS examined during any audit—whether it is preliminary, a final registration or surveillance). Interestingly, this improvement cycle appears to begin with a static document of procedures, but the various ways of exploring the defined procedures will allow for addressing the inefficiencies and discovering the root causes of a problem. In spite of the outward symbolism of receiving a certificate indicating successful inspection of the written procedures, the fundamental nature of the ISO 9000 effort will be the quality impact it has on everyone in the organization.

9. EVEN THOUGH ISO 9000 REQUIRES REGULAR AUDITS, DOES ANYONE EVER LOSE THEIR REGISTRATION STATUS?

There have been several instances where ISO 9000 registered organizations have lost their status. The most recent involved a company which had changed management, and the new management abandoned the company's quality system. Generally speaking, though, it is a rare occurrence.

10. IS ISO 9000 A COMPLEX, CUMBERSOME, BUREAUCRATIC PROCESS THAT WAS WRITTEN BY PEOPLE OUT OF TOUCH WITH THE BUSINESS WORLD?

The basic (and simplistic) nature of ISO 9000 often takes registered companies by surprise. Most find that, with the exception of third-party audits, it cannot be differentiated from the quality system itself (which is the purpose of the standard). At times, it can be bureaucratic, but if handled correctly, ISO 9000 will not prove to be burdensome.

11. WILL AN ISO 9000 REGISTRATION ELIMINATE ALL CUSTOMER AUDITS?

Possibly—some ISO 9000 registered companies have reported a dramatic decrease in the number of customer quality audits, e.g., one manufacturer reported that they had been receiving 67 audits annually (with three full-time employees charged with managing the plant visits.) After ISO 9000, the number of customer audits dropped in half, allowing two of the employees to be reassigned. Others have reported drops in the 15% - 20% range.

Not all companies report the same level of reductions; however, a successful ISO 9000 registration should result in easier and quicker second-party audits.

A slightly different view emphasizes that there is a desire to reduce the number of customer audits, BUT not necessarily the number of customer visits. Having the basic quality fundamentals addressed by ISO 9000 will allow for more in-depth examination of quality-related issues, e.g., waste reduction, on-time handling, inventory reduction, turn around, etc.

12. THE MOST COMPELLING REASON FOR ISO 9000 HAS BEEN COMPETITIVE (HAVING A POSITIVE MARKETING ADVANTAGE OR MINIMIZING A NEGATIVE POSITION). IS THIS CORRECT?

Generally speaking, most companies that have completed a successful ISO 9000 registration have found that the internal benefits and improvements have far outweighed the competitive rationale. Many companies have cited overwhelming positive statistics as a result of ISO 9000, e.g., the percentage of products meeting specifications has increased, on-time deliveries have increased, first-time approval rates have increased, waste has decreased, and outdated equipment has been removed.

13. WILL MY CUSTOMERS REQUIRE ISO 9000?

In many cases, this is absolutely true. Some industries are reporting, however, that the situation is reversed and it's the suppliers who are actually pushing the customer. This is not all that bad. For, in reality, what is occurring is a quality partnership which is a "win-win" situation. There have been numerous examples of customers both asking and requiring ISO 9000 (private and governmental purchases) and, interestingly, many companies have been educating their customers on ISO 9000 and its benefits.

14. IS ISO 9000 BEING REQUIRED OF COMPANIES'
SUPPLIERS?

Most companies today are encouraging their suppliers to get registered or else are stating that the requirement is coming — but
have not yet established a time frame or absolute date. Clearly,
the time will come when a company, in attempting to select between two suppliers (all other things being equal), will give the
edge to the ISO 9000-registered supplier.

15. WHAT IS THE REAL VALUE OF AN ISO 9000
REGISTRATION?

Read the next chapter in this book.

4
WHY IS ISO 9000 NECESSARY?

What is the value of seeking an ISO 9000 registration? Is it really necessary? How much business have we lost by not being registered, or how much business will we lose if we're not registered?

These and other similar questions have been raised from the very first moment ISO 9000 appeared on the scene. In most cases, careful analysis of worldwide business conditions have led companies to decide that ISO 9000 efforts made sense. Starting in early 1990, it was clear that the European Community would be enacting measures which would make ISO 9000 a condition of doing business, and by January 1992, two events occurred which dramatically altered the perception of ISO 9000. First, the European Community published their "ISO 9000 directives" which indicated that the ISO 9000 quality standards would be a condition of doing business by January 1993. Second, many companies' competitors were engaged in the pursuit of ISO 9000, and they were beginning to publish their successes in obtaining registration.

As ISO 9000 has evolved, it has become evident that there are seven fundamental reasons why it makes sense to pursue registration:

1. INTERNATIONAL CUSTOMERS ARE REQUIRING
   COMPLIANCE

There has been an increasing number of customer requests for companies to provide formal proof of the quality process used to design, develop and support commercial offerings. This is certainly the case in Europe, where the European Community has aggressively embraced the ISO 9000 standards series for almost all types of commercially traded products and services; including hardware, software, processed materials and services. Many European companies (customers) are making conformance to ISO 9000 standards a condition in purchasing agreements. However, ISO 9000 is not limited solely to the European marketplace. It is beginning to grow in acceptance worldwide. Today, the ISO 9000 standards provide a common baseline for meeting the quality requirements of products and services traded in over 80 countries around the world; a number which may eventually climb to more than 100 countries (Appendix 2).

Currently, many people are not aware of the variations regarding an ISO 9000 registration (9001 vs 9002; registering only one location or part of a location; only registering an overseas facility and taking credit for ISO 9000 across the entire company, etc). However, as the ISO 9000 movement increases and customers become more aware, it is certain that the requirements for compliance will become more stringent and demanding—a fact that should only work to the benefit of those companies successfully meeting the demands of an ISO 9000 registration.

2. INTERNATIONAL GOVERNMENT REGULATIONS FOR
   PROCUREMENT REQUIRE ISO 9000 COMPLIANCE

In April 1991, the European Economic Commission issued a series of directives which indicated that conformance to the ISO 9000 quality standards would be a prerequisite for doing business in the European Common Market by 1993. However, it turns out that these directives were not taken literally by the majority of the European member countries, and an across-the-board requirement for ISO 9000 has not yet materialized.

Instead, there have been specific instances of European government agencies utilizing ISO 9000 as a business requirement. For example, in the UK, the Ministry of Defence has made it MANDATORY for all suppliers wishing to do business with them (effective September 1993!); and the purchasing arms of the Italian and German governments have been issuing bids with ISO 9000 registration as part of their contractual conditions.

Outside the EEC, there have been requirements from several countries such as India, Mexico, China, Venezuela, Thailand and Canada.

Since most of the member nations of the International Organization for Standardization have already adopted ISO 9000 as their national quality standard, it is reasonable to assume that many of these countries' purchasing agencies will be requiring ISO 9000 compliance as a normal matter of course.

3. COMPETITIVE PRESSURES

The companies that have attained ISO 9000 registration use it as a marketing advantage and have pointed this out to prospective customers. The companies not having achieved ISO 9000 compliance strive to minimize ISO 9000—and its effects on total quality. Eventually, the customer will decide which position is appropriate and will act accordingly. Individual companies will have to decide if their respective customers will be making purchasing decisions based on ISO 9000 attainment. (One of the best ways to determine this will be to ask them!)

Although competition is a strong reason for embarking on an ISO 9000 effort, it appears that many of the competitive advantages of registration may be disappearing. Just about every industry has been penetrated by ISO 9000 registrants (somewhere around the world); and many companies are pursuing a strategy which will lead them to register all of their worldwide facilities.

By year end 1995, the expectation is at least 90,000+ registrations worldwide, with a corresponding United States number of approximately 8,000+. (Indications are that currently 30,000+ U.S. companies are in the pipeline—working toward an ISO 9000 registration). The numbers appear to be growing exponentially, and worldwide estimates for the year 2000 are in the range of 200,000 to 250,000.

4. PARTICIPATION IN JOINT VENTURES

There is an emerging, relatively new occurrence among companies that have already achieved ISO 9000 compliance. For want of a better term, I call this the "Fraternal Initiation Phenomenon." It involves companies that do the necessary things to achieve a successful ISO 9000 registration (install controls, document their procedures, make sure everyone in their organization understands and follows these practices, perform the necessary internal audits to satisfy everyone - including the third-party assessors or registrars and, finally, complete a successful ISO 9000 registration). At this point, having passed the "ISO 9000 initiation," the company turns to its suppliers and "requires" ISO 9000 from them. They are, in effect, saying, "I have gone through the trials and tribulations to achieve this quality level. I know what it means as well as what it doesn't mean; BUT overall I believe it is a good thing and I would like to have the same degree of confidence that YOU are doing what you say you are doing in the quality area." Although companies have been dealing with their suppliers for many years, the ISO 9000 certificate is another (standard) way to strengthen the bonds and provide the quality assurance in business relationships.

As more companies embark on the ISO 9000 trail, and as more individuals become comfortable with the extent and significance of adherence to the ISO 9000 quality standards, there will be an increasing emphasis on providing assurance to all of your business partners and alliances.

It is also interesting to note the appearance of a "Cascade Effect" when dealing with ISO 9000. Most customers are aware that companies seldom provide the totality of the goods or services themselves. In fact, the 1990's is often characterized as the decade of partnerships, alliances, joint activities, etc. Thus, the more knowledgeable customers are requesting ISO 9000 compliance from not only the main provider (or general contractor) but from all of the providers in the chain (e.g., secondary, tertiary, etc.) who play a role in bringing the ultimate product or service to the marketplace. Clearly, if any of the contributors along the supply chain fail in terms of quality, the end product or service will be tainted, and a less than satisfactory perception will result.

5. ISO 9000 IS A GOOD FOUNDATION FOR BUILDING
   A QUALITY PROGRAM

Inherent in seeking an ISO 9000 registration is that an organization must take the time to formulate and understand what its key quality processes are; must ensure that these processes are implemented and followed by everyone in the organization; and must take care that supporting quality records are documented and maintained in order to demonstrate conformance to an outside agency. Performing these actions will result in the achieving and sustaining of specified quality levels in a CONSISTENT and REPEATABLE manner.

Many organizations have not implemented good quality programs, and thus an ISO 9000 effort can provide the basis or foundation for establishing desired quality practices. It is fundamentally simple, and for this reason establishes a "bedrock" which improves any operation in the company. ISO 9000 does not require any esoteric or unnatural actions; it merely asks that you document what you do. The mere act of putting down on paper, or on-line, the processes and procedures employed in the name of quality, actually results in numerous benefits.

Although ISO 9000 is not a total quality management approach, it does contain some elements which are generally not found in many TQM programs (e.g., calibration of equipment, training records, etc.). It can complement existing quality efforts by filling in some of the missing pieces. It will focus on the specifics of what people actually do, and this will lead to various quality system improvements such as locating flaws in the procedures, eliminating duplications within parallel operations and closing the gaps between various procedures and processes.

In spite of the various quality efforts in existence, many companies do not have any idea of their quality processes, and the ISO 9000 effort is one way to get focus! The press is replete with stories about how ISO 9000 has assisted companies in starting on the quality trail and for many, this is the push needed to apply the proper attention to this vital area.

6. ISO 9000 COMPLEMENTS AN EXISTING QUALITY
   PROGRAM

By linking the ISO 9000 program to your quality efforts, several benefits will accrue within your various organizations. Filling in some of the missing gaps and providing focus on the "nitty-gritty" of what people actually do leads to various quality system improvements. This is especially true in light of recent corporate "down sizing" efforts which often result in the loss of both people and responsibilities. Having a documented and well understood trail enables those organizations to withstand some of the impacts and to be in a better position to sustain and grow.

There appears to be a one-way relationship between ISO 9000 and many TQM efforts (e.g., the Malcolm Baldrige National Quality Award — see Chapter 10). For example, if you did not have any type of quality program in existence, a successful ISO 9000 registration would probably only be worth approximately 300-350 points on a Baldrige rating. This is due to the fact that there is some overlap between ISO 9000 and several of the seven Baldrige categories. However, ISO 9000 does not emphasize two areas "Results" and

"Customer Satisfaction," which represents 50% of the total available points on the Baldrige scale. Thus, ISO 9000, by itself, represents only a start on the quality journey.

Interestingly, it is possible to be a Baldrige winner and still have trouble passing an ISO 9000 audit. This is due to the fact that ISO 9000 asks for many things that are not looked at by a Baldrige examiner. Thus, if these areas are ignored, the ISO 9000 assessment would be lacking.

Using both together, however, is the best solution. ISO 9000 provides the basis or foundation of a good quality effort. It forces one to focus on the basics, document the procedures and maintain suitable records to demonstrate proof. Baldrige (or any TQM effort) can build on this foundation and direct the efforts to improving the established processes, benchmarking them against best of breed, enhancing the basics to reduce cycle time, focusing on the market needs, etc.

7. ISO 9000 IS CONDUCIVE TO EMPLOYEE
EMPOWERMENT

Many companies have seen a significant amount of employee support and enthusiasm for their ISO 9000 program. Most organizations that have initiated ISO 9000 report that their employees have bought into the program and are pleased with the results. (Not all employees, but empirical studies indicate a significant proportion of the work force). There appear to be several reasons for this phenomenon:

A) Quality, at best, often uses terms and ideas which do not always translate to one's work place ("6 sigma," "100x," "Zero Defect," etc.). Although the terms help convey the strategy and direction to be employed, it is sometimes difficult for many employees to take these concepts back to their work stations and determine how they can comply. ISO 9000, on the other hand, merely requires that each employee document what it is they do, and then maintain the necessary records to be in a position to demonstrate that they actually do what they say they are doing. This simple task has the benefit of bringing the abstract concept of quality down to the "do-er." An elaborate translation is not necessary. Once the connection is made, people can see how their individual contribution can play a part in the "whole" of a company's quality thrust.

B) Having taken the time to document the realities of a job and then analyze the results to fill in the gaps, eliminate the redundancies, and identify and correct the flaws, the resulting documented processes provide a basis for understanding where and how a person fits into the total equation. It is easy to see how one person can make a difference and just how their respective contribution can influence the results of the total entity. It's basic and fundamental, but it is this simplicity which is the key, and just about all who have gone through the ISO 9000 program have experienced similar results.

C) Employees are EMPOWERED! By asking them to document the realities of their jobs, these employees put down the "what should be" rather than the "what is" or the "what was." In most cases, the person doing the job is in the best position to determine the right way things should be done and the process of requiring employees to document their quality actions has produced some interesting and pleasantly surprising results.

BENEFITS OF AN ISO 9000 REGISTRATION EFFORT

Unlimited numbers of testimonials extol the benefits of having gone through the ISO 9000 experience. Although many aspects have proven to be overly burdensome, in general, the consensus has indicated positive feedback. It turns out that the majority of the benefits come from the PLANNING, PREPARATION, and INTERNAL AUDIT aspects of the implementation. In most cases, the external registrar (auditor) merely serves to confirm your own findings.

Most companies have profited from activities aimed at resolving their non-conformances. Leveraging your results across a wide spectrum of your organization will allow you to provide benefits which are greater than the sum of the individual pieces.

The most obvious benefits (Figure 4.1) will occur in terms of defining authority and clear identification of responsibility for all your key operations. Coupled with these results will be the discipline to maintain your processes through all of their change/modification activities which are a normal part of the business cycle. Basically, your employees will be able to demonstrate adherence to execution and attainment of quality criteria for their respective responsibilities. Many companies have been able to effect a series of improvements through the continuous monitoring of corrective actions. The benefits appear to group within two categories: namely those that are realized internally and the benefits that accrue in terms of external factors.

The INTERNAL BENEFITS include:

Better organizational definition and architecture
Greater quality awareness throughout the company
Better documentation of your procedures/practices
Increased control of your operations
Constant analysis of and solution to problems
Positive cultural change

The EXTERNAL BENEFITS include:

Higher perceived quality of your company's goods and services
Competitive edge in quality decisions
Improvement in customer satisfaction
Increase in market opportunities
Reduction in the number of customer quality audits
Quicker response to quality-oriented solicitations

ISO 9000 BENEFITS

1. ESTABLISHES DOCUMENTED PROCESSES

2. CREATES DISCIPLINE TO MAINTAIN PROCESSES

3. DEFINES **AUTHORITY** & **RESPONSIBILITY**

4. DEMONSTRATES:

   • ADHERENCE TO EXECUTION

   • ATTAINMENT OF QUALITY CRITERIA

5. ALIGNMENT OF SKILLS TO JOB REQUIREMENTS

6. CONTINUOUS MONITORING AND IMPROVEMENT THROUGH
   CORRECTIVE ACTION PROCEDURES

FIGURE 4.1

The backbone of the entire ISO 9000 program has proven to be the combination of MANAGEMENT REVIEWS, an aggressive INTERNAL AUDIT PROGRAM, and a focus on the CORRECTIVE ACTION PROGRAM. Together, they have substantially improved companies' operations and resulted in an increase in the overall quality effort.

One of the more interesting by-products of the ISO 9000 experience has been the impact on employee morale. Substantial gains have been noted in quality awareness, quality participation (active involvement), and quality of work as well as a general improvement in overall TEAMWORK and FOCUS. (Figure 4.2)

ISO 9000 IMPACT

The decision to bring ISO 9000 into an organization will also require that the company incur additional expenses in time, energy and money. There are actual out-of-pocket costs as well as people time and effort. The magnitude of the ISO 9000 costs will be proportional to the relative size of your company and will generally encompass three distinct areas:

1. REGISTRAR ASSOCIATED EXPENSES (the smallest of the costs)

The audit fees (application fees, desk-check fees, preliminary audit fees, final assessment fees, certificate issuance fees, travel and living expenses for the auditors, registration fees, etc.). The magnitude of these charges will differ across the spectrum of registrars and it's best to understand the nature and scope of the charges before embarking on an ISO 9000 journey. In this context, it will pay to shop around. Also refer to Chapter 8, "Registrars and Consultants" for additional insights. The magnitude should be under 10% of the total cost to achieve ISO 9000 compliance.

RESULTS OF AN EMPLOYEE MORALE SURVEY
(Percentage of Positive Responses)

	January 1992 (Before ISO 9000)	December 1992 (After ISO 9000)	Delta
Employee "Buy-In:"			
Company's Quality Strategy	69%	80.1%	+11.1
Personal Progress on Quality	40%	84.9%	+44.9
Employee's Own Participation:			
Active Involvement in Quality	74%	81.6%	+ 7.6
Quality of Work	64%	81.2%	+17.2
Employee's Perception of Management Involvement:			
Immediate Manager Demonstrates Commitment to Quality	58%	74.2%	+16.2
Senior Management Demonstrates Commitment to Quality	37%	67.5%	+30.5

FIGURE 4.2

2. EXTERNAL PREPARATIONS (medium level costs)

Items such as educational expenses (materials, classes, etc.), the cost of the ISO 9000 standards themselves and other related expenses such as the use of consultants or advisers, supporting tools or aids (on-line systems, documentation control packages, error control systems, process controls, etc.). In many cases, these costs are optional and they will vary based on your own particular needs and capabilities. In order to control these costs, many smaller companies have banded together and have, through their joint efforts, been able to keep these costs from growing too large.

3. INTERNAL COSTS (potentially the largest of the three areas, representing approximately 90% of the total)

Included within this category are the people-related expenses for actually performing the implementation, the training and the required internal audits. ISO 9000 is an explicit process which requires an amount of detailed conformance (i.e., you must address all of the required elements). This requirement will have the largest impact in your organization, as it will affect ALL of your personnel to some degree. The impact on your people will, of course, vary by entity (depending on the type of work being performed, the degree of established procedures, the level of documentation, the quality awareness and participation, etc.). Although this category represents the largest amount of expense associated with the establishment of an ISO 9000 effort, recognize that these costs are generally a one-time expense and, once registration status is achieved, these expenses will drop considerably.

On the positive side, the return on investment will be quite pleasing. Most companies have reported that they have realized paybacks in one to three years, with the majority of these gains coming from error reductions, increased first-pass yields, elimination of waste, cycle time reductions, elimination of unnecessary practices, reductions in overall operating procedures, improvements in on-time deliveries, etc.

These gains are not limited to just the first year, but appear to be continuous. Viewed in this light, the investment in ISO 9000 can realistically show dramatic returns for the long term.

5 THE ISO 9000 FAMILY

ISO 9000 is a family of high-level models used to implement and assess quality management and quality assurance systems.

The ISO 9000 series of standards consists of a series of documents which were originally published in 1987 and subsequently revised in 1994. The revisions and changes are highlighted in Appendix 12): See Figure 5.1 for an outline of the series.

- GUIDELINES:
    ISO 9000
    ISO 9004

- REQUIREMENTS:
    ISO 9001
    ISO 9002
    ISO 9003

ISO 9000 PUBLICATIONS

Quality Management & Quality Assurance
Standards - Guidelines for Selection
and Use

Quality Management and Quality
System Elements - Guidelines

Quality Systems - Model for Quality
Assurance in Design, Development,
Production, Installation, and Servicing

Quality Sytems - Model for Quality
Assurance in Production, Installation, and
Servicing

Quality Systems - Model for Quality
Assurance in Final Inspection and Test

FIGURE 5.1

The ISO 9000 and ISO 9004 documents offer guidance and interpretation, while the ISO 9001, ISO 9002 and ISO 9003 publications are the actual requirements or auditable standards. In each case, the ISO 9000 family targets a supplier's ability to assure conformance to a buyer's specified quality requirements (sometimes these are contractually stated) (Figure 5.2). Basically, a company will choose to register to one of the three requirement models (ISO 9001, ISO 9002 or ISO 9003) as a reflection of its business. The other documents in the ISO 9000 family are useful in providing understanding and interpretation of the various quality terms and philosophies.

GUIDELINES AND REQUIREMENTS

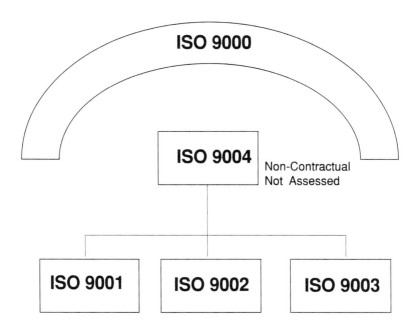

FIGURE 5.2

ISO 9000   is a guideline document which aids the user in appropriately selecting among the three standards, ISO 9001, ISO 9002, ISO 9003, by clarifying the various quality-oriented concepts and terms and defining the relationships of these objectives.

ISO 9004   is a guideline document for the use and application of the standards in quality management and quality-system elements.

ISO 9001   is a series of requirements which apply to the design, development, production, service and installation processes in order to demonstrate a supplier's capabilities.

ISO 9002   is a series of requirements which encompass production, installation, and servicing, in order to demonstrate a supplier's capabilities. (In 1987, the original version did not include "Design Control" and "Servicing," but in the 1994 version only "Design Control" has been omitted).

ISO 9003   is a series of requirements which only pertain to the areas of final inspection and test.

ISO 9001, the most comprehensive of the three auditable standards, delineates quality system requirements into the following 20 categories:

1. MANAGEMENT RESPONSIBILITY

    management's establishment of a clear, concise quality policy that reflects corporate goals

2. QUALITY SYSTEM

    creation of a quality system that is thoroughly documented and followed

3. CONTRACT REVIEW
consists of review processes and the ability to satisfy customer requirements

4. DESIGN CONTROL
general concerns, design/development planning, input/output stages, verification, validation and implementation changes

5. DOCUMENT AND DATA CONTROL
methods to ensure consistency and timeliness

6. PURCHASING
maintaining clear and complete data and verification of purchased products

7. CONTROL OF CUSTOMER-SUPPLIED PRODUCT
notifying the customer regarding damage, loss, defect, etc.

8. PRODUCT IDENTIFICATION AND TRACEABILITY
clear identification to establish a correlation between a product and its design/production documentation

9. PROCESS CONTROL
covers production within a manufacturing environment and activities connected to performing an actual service within a service organization

10. INSPECTION AND TESTING
ensures that all material is verified and satisfactory

11. CONTROL OF INSPECTION, MEASURING, AND
TEST EQUIPMENT

> ensures all test equipment is current, labeled, verified, and accurate

12. INSPECTION AND TEST STATUS

> concentrates on inspection status identification methods

13. CONTROL OF NONCONFORMING PRODUCT

> reviews control, identification, and proper handling techniques

14. CORRECTIVE AND PREVENTIVE ACTION

> investigating nonconforming products, distinguishing isolated errors and system problems, modifying existing systems, and deciding on the implementation of actions and followup plans

15. HANDLING, STORAGE, PACKAGING, PRESERVATION, AND
DELIVERY

> ensuring safety of personnel through proper handling, securing, storage areas, responsibilities, and suitable goods for delivery

16. CONTROL OF QUALITY RECORDS

> determining the achievement of customer-level quality

17. INTERNAL QUALITY AUDITS

> efficiency and effectiveness of the quality system

18. TRAINING

> evaluation of employee qualifications and skills

19. SERVICING
   customer receives desired benefits when buying the goods/service

20. STATISTICAL TECHNIQUES
   monitoring and evaluating the quality system

*ISO 9002 covers 19 of these 20 elements:
   Omitting Category Number 4 - Design Control

*ISO 9003 covers 16 of these 20 elements:
   Omitting: Category Number 4   - Design Control
                  Category Number 6   - Purchasing
                  Category Number 9   - Process Control
                  Category Number 19 - Servicing

The following is a summary description of each of the 20 categories contained in ISO 9001:

1. MANAGEMENT RESPONSIBILITY

Covers the establishment of a quality policy (including the objectives and commitment) and the effective communication of the policy throughout the organization. The quality policy reflects the corporate goals as well as the motivation to develop and maintain the appropriate systems for achieving the goals. A good policy should be clear, concise, and encompass specifics such as performance, availability, reliability, customer interests, etc.

The idea of communicating the policy to everyone will ensure understanding and create ways for people to relate it to their roles and responsibilities.

Also included within this section are organizational responsibilities and authority, the verification of resources (and personnel), management reviews, and (optionally, depending on the size of the organization) the establishment of a management representative for quality assurance.

2. QUALITY SYSTEM

The creation of a quality system must not only be compliant with the elements of the standard, but should be thoroughly documented and followed. The behavioral assessment of implementation is always performed against the quality system documentation only, and never against the standard itself. This may affect functions which specify requirements in excess of the ISO 9000 standards and will, therefore, be assessed against the more demanding elements.

3. CONTRACT REVIEW

There will be various interpretations of this element depending upon the nature of the business as well as the customer's contractual demands. In addition to the review process itself (which will be a planned, documented and fully embellished system allowing for appropriate record keeping), the organization must assess its ability to satisfy the purchaser's requirements (e.g., stock vs. delivery schedules or elaborate financial reviews).

4. DESIGN CONTROL

This is one of the most important of the ISO 9001 elements and reflects the thought that a product's ultimate quality is determined at this juncture. The Design Control section covers general concerns, design and development planning (including organizational interfaces and the assignment of various activities), the input stage, the output stage, the verification (reviews, etc.), the validation and the methods for implementing changes (which, of course, should contain provisions for customers to supply feedback).

5. DOCUMENT AND DATA CONTROL

Since documentation plays a vital role in the entire process, the manner and methods used to ensure consistency and timeliness are key. The rules for document control will vary (according to the specifics and use of the document), but what is of paramount importance is the responsibility for approval and the subsequent control which governs the process. It goes without saying that these rules, themselves, are documented.

6. PURCHASING

The concept of purchasing (specifically subcontracting) is, in reality, an extension of the various activities and processes performed by the organization in developing, producing, distributing and servicing a product. Although ISO 9000 does not explicitly require a subcontractor to have an ISO 9000 registration, the implication exists. This section also deals with maintaining clear and complete purchasing data, along with the assessment of subcontractors as to their ability to perform.

The verification of the purchased product (either at the source or upon receipt) is also a vital aspect to the process. However, it should be noted that the supplier is ultimately responsible for quality, regardless of the results of the verification process.

7. CONTROL OF CUSTOMER-SUPPLIED PRODUCT

This element deals with notifying the customer regarding damage, defect or loss, as well as such things as physically separating unsuitable goods. It may stand alone as a separate element or be included within the provisions for the proper handling, identification and storage of all products.

8. PRODUCT IDENTIFICATION AND TRACEABILITY

Clearly, identification must establish a correlation between a product and its design/production documentation. This should not be construed as a labeling methodology, but rather should establish a relationship with specific drawings or other technical specifications. As with the other elements of the standard, the resultant processes must be thoroughly documented.

9. PROCESS CONTROL

The word "process" is used in a broad context. For a manufacturing environment it would mean production, while for service industries it covers all activities connected with performing the actual service itself. The issues addressed in this section comprise production planning, environment, equipment, technology, process control, work instructions, product characteristics control, criteria for workmanship, etc. It is the only section of the standard that deals directly with production activities. The production plan must define, document and communicate all manufacturing processes and inspection points. There must also be a clear method for establishing that a manufacturing process or inspection has been satisfactorily completed.

Equipment and machines should be regularly maintained and checked for performance and accuracy, and there should preferably be a maintenance plan and records. Some equipment may also need to be specifically approved and/or calibrated. Misplaced or otherwise unavailable equipment operation and maintenance manuals are often a source of noncompliance with this section of the standard.

Minimum qualifications for workmen and operators performing specific processes should be predetermined. In addition, clear work instructions and process procedures must be directly available at relevant work stations. These instructions may be in the form of manuals, posted notices, notes on drawings, etc. Whenever the lack of such instructions could adversely affect quality, the standard requires that they be established and be available at appropriate work stations.

The work instructions and process procedures may only be issued by an authorized party, must be periodically checked for current relevance, and their placement, removal and revision should be controlled.

10. INSPECTION AND TESTING

One of the relevant aspects of this section is that all received material (which is planned to be in the final product) must be verified. If the inspection program at the source is deemed to be satisfactory and the products have suitable records, the verification of incoming products can be a review and recording procedure. This section also deals with the "in-process" procedures as well as final inspection and testing. As is the case with the other elements, every inspection must be supported with a record.

11. CONTROL OF INSPECTION, MEASURING, AND TEST EQUIPMENT

The key words in this section are "controlled" and "calibrated." If one had to choose the area which gives the most difficulty in the development and production environment, this would be the one. On the other hand, by focusing attention in this vital area, one is able to correct anomalies and tighten the controls. Ensuring that all test equipment is current, labeled, verified and accurate, along with maintaining the required documentation, is the key to success.

12. INSPECTION AND TEST STATUS

This area concentrates on inspection status identification. Tagging, labeling, color coding, bar coding, etc. are suggestions for addressing this element.

13. CONTROL OF NONCONFORMING PRODUCT

Control, identification and proper handling techniques should be coupled with appropriate reviews (for final disposition). In some cases, the purchaser may actually require a report of the nonconformities and, therefore, a procedure to handle this eventuality should exist.

14. CORRECTIVE AND PREVENTIVE ACTION

The main distinction between a useful, efficient and productive quality system and a bureaucratic one is the handling of corrective actions. Investigation and analysis of nonconforming conditions and dealing with causes to prevent reurrance is how quality assurance becomes productive and profitable. Inspection and segregation of a nonconforming product is also important, but does not, in itself, contribute to an increase of overall productivity. The fastest and perhaps surest way to evaluate a quality system is through correction actions which will eliminate causes of actual nonconformities and preventive actions which will eliminate the causes of "potential" nonconformities. The first step that must be taken is to investigate the cause of a nonconformity. Distinction should be drawn between isolated errors and system problems. Correction of a system or process problem may require changes on many levels, including the modification of product design, changes to manufacturing equipment, personnel training, revision of procedures, etc. Errors can be usually corrected on the local level where they occurred. The next step is a decision as to what corrective actions are required and the subsequent implementation of these actions. The last step in handling corrective actions is a followup to ascertain that the actions are effective. Checking on effectiveness is often overlooked and, most often, not documented. The standard explicitly requires that effectiveness of the corrective actions must be verified.

15. HANDLING, STORAGE, PACKAGING, PRESERVATION, AND DELIVERY

Handling should deal with the physical aspects as well as ensure the safety of the personnel and the product. As a consequence of the actions, appropriate levels of training will be required (see Section 18 of this chapter on Training).

Storage areas should be secure, the movement of goods should be controlled and the on-hand stocks must be regularly assessed. Appropriate segregation methods and procedures for dealing with exceptions are essential.

Packaging is treated like other production-oriented processes. On a general level, packaging should spell out authority and responsibility, while at a more detailed level, specific work instructions are required. This will also hold true for the preservation aspects, especially when the supplier controls the products or goods in question. Depending on whether or not delivery is part of the operation, the standard notes that the supplier has the responsibility to provide goods suitable for the intended means of delivery.

16. CONTROL OF QUALITY RECORDS

Basically, these records demonstrate that the customer-required level of quality has been achieved. This particular section is the broadest in coverage, being referenced by almost every other element. The records themselves must be identifiable, legible, easily retrievable, stored appropriately and retained for a specified period of time.

When using a record maintenance system, the emphasis should be on the retrievability aspects. This is another section which, if not properly addressed, can cause numerous problems during the audits.

17. INTERNAL QUALITY AUDITS

Internal auditing, corrective actions and followups are the mechanisms by which a quality system can change and become more efficient and profitable. The first requirement is the establishment and implementation of a comprehensive system of planned and documented quality audits. Comprehensive means that every activity required by the standard must be included. Generally, the audit plan is actually based on sections and subsections of the standard. The purpose of the audits is to verify compliance with the documented system and to determine the effectiveness of the quality system. Determination of effectiveness is included in order that the quality auditor will go beyond the simple verification as to whether things are being done according to the rules and, in fact, assess effectiveness of the rules themselves. Effectiveness is the ultimate goal, while adherence to rules is only the means to achieve this goal.

Internal audits must be conducted on a regularly established schedule. Generally, one year should be the maximum period of time that can be allowed between two consecutive audits for any given activity. The one-year rule should be supplemented by provisions for increasing the frequency of auditing to account for the relative importance of an activity or in reaction to recurring problems. Half-yearly or even quarterly auditing should be encouraged at the early stages of implementing a new system. An audit plan that just specifies yearly intervals for all activities, without any variation in the implementation period, is a clear indication that there is no serious commitment to the overall quality system.

The audit procedures should call for the establishment of an audit plan, assignment of auditors, state auditor qualification requirements, describe preparations for auditing, set rules for the audit itself, specify reporting formats and provide for the distribution of the audit reports.

Finally, the written audit reports must be compiled and communicated to the responsible people. Audit reports generally report findings in terms of nonconformances or noncompliances. Every nonconformance must be responded to by a corrective action and then re-audited to verify effectiveness.

18. TRAINING

A vital aspect of this element is the degree of analysis which will be used to determine an organization's training needs, especially as they relate to their key processes. In addition to delineating the training requirements, every employee must have defined qualifications and training records which will enable them to do their jobs. One of the most frequent questions asked by auditors is, "How do you know that individual is qualified to do the job." The most effective way to deal with this inquiry is through the use of a well-documented and current set of training records. Lastly, the establishment of the effectiveness of the prescribed training will provide both insight and awareness of areas for improvement.

19. SERVICING

One way to understand the servicing element is that it requires an understanding of the product being produced. Servicing operations should meet all the requirements of the whole standard. This section is, in fact, only a reminder and reinforcement of the more general requirements.

The end product of a service is the desired benefit that the customer specified when purchasing the service. The actual production of a service is the performance of all activities and functions required to achieve the desired benefit, while a process is the individual activity or function. Conceptually, the servicing element differs very little from the manufacturing environment, except that the processes do not always result in a physical modification of a material product. Production of a service should be planned in the same manner as required for production of material goods.

The actions of inspection and testing are the verification that the service has been completed in accordance with a documented plan and/or that benefits of the service are in compliance with the "specified benefits." For example, in the case of maintenance, verification consists of checking that all specified activities have been performed satisfactorily, while for a repair, the verification would normally require testing for proper operation.

20. STATISTICAL TECHNIQUES

The standard does not contain any specific requirements with regard to the use of statistical techniques. It merely states that they should be documented and used where required.

If the nature of the processes and/or the product warrants the use of statistical techniques, the supplier should include (in the process control and/or inspection procedures) a reference to an appropriate standard or rules for application of the statistical techniques.

ISO 9000 ADDITIONAL GUIDELINES

The ISO 9000 standards cover the quality processes to produce any or all products and services. Being so broadly focused, they offer no details about their application to specific domains or expertise. Consequently, the ISO 9000 series contains additional guideline documents (for selected and specific areas such as ISO 9000-3 for Software, ISO 9004-2 for Service and ISO 9004-3 for Processed Materials). For example, a software development company would have to spend a considerable amount of time and energy evaluating the ISO 9000-3 software guidance document (as well as "TICKIT"). A more definitive discussion of both of these subjects can be found in Appendix 6. (For a complete listing of the current set of ISO 9000 manuals, please refer to Appendix 13).

ISO 9001, ISO 9002, ISO 9003 — WHICH IS APPROPRIATE?

It is common knowledge that it takes anywhere from 6 months to 2 years for a location to get ready and be registered, depending on the starting status. Numerous United States companies are presently proceeding to get their development activities in order, but they probably will not achieve ISO 9000 in the immediate future. Thus, their initial marketing approach will be to convince customers/suppliers on a one-to-one basis that their quality system is at least equivalent to the ISO 9000 criteria. It is not clear that customers will find this approach acceptable over the long term, especially if they have other choices.

In addition to your customers, your competitors will be in the process of registering their facilities (to either 9001, 9002 or 9003 depending upon the nature of their business and what they perform at their respective sites). Therefore, to remain competitive and even take a competitive lead, it is in your best interests to register according to your own operational objectives.

The fundamental difference between ISO 9001 and ISO 9002 is whether to include "Design Control" as part of the scope of registration. Some companies are quoted as saying that they aren't in the business of selling their design activity, therefore they are only interested in seeking ISO 9002 certificates. The confusion caused by this remark results from misinterpreting and misunderstanding the ISO 9001 registration process, as well as the implication that the design capabilities will somehow be jeopardized by including these acitvities within the scope of an ISO 9000 registration.

Most companies are proud of their design and development activities and, by registering them appropriately, they will be able to demonstrate that their design and development processes can achieve the level of quality assurance that is outlined in the ISO 9001 standards. In addition, these companies would endeavor to demonstrate that their processes far surpassed the requirements spelled out in the ISO 9000 set of standards and that their logo represented a level of quality assurance in excess of the worldwide minimum.

There have also been some allegations regarding registrars dictating which level a site should seek for registration of its operations. This has been expressed as the registrar "...making us strive for 9001 or for 9002." However, this is simply not the case! As a potential registeree, you define the scope and purpose of the evaluation. The registrar is hired to perform an audit, nothing more and nothing less. You determine where and how the ISO 9000 activity is to take place. You determine whether to go for 9001, 9002 or 9003. You include certain areas and exclude others. If a registrar is dictating these elements, then a grievous error is being made.

The ISO 9000 process is designed to assist you in becoming more aware of quality assurance and to provide a mechanism for your customers to be assured that quality processes are in place and that you are "doing what you say you are doing." By concentrating your focus on the elements of the standard, you will find gaps in your procedures, some duplications and some flaws. You will also be in a position to enact improvements and efficiencies. This will ultimately lead to a cycle of continuous improvement and, hopefully, result in better quality.

Figure 5.3 indicates the relationship of the various elements of the ISO 9000 system. In the first stage, a company will develop their quality manual, which is the result of establishing the appropriate quality controls and providing the necessary documentation and records to substantiate these control procedures ("Say what you do"). The next phase is the evaluation aspect, which requires a substantial amount of time and energy devoted to conducting numerous internal assessments. This phase will provide sufficient information for a company to demonstrate that they are, in truth, "doing what they say they are doing." During this stage in the overall approach, companies will learn the most about their strengths and weaknesses. The evaluation will also show how good the resultant quality system is and where additional emphasis may have to be placed. The next phase involves bringing in the external (third-party) auditor or registrar, who will assess the company's quality manual and stated quality processes against the company's actual performance ("Show Me").

ISO 9000 PROCESS

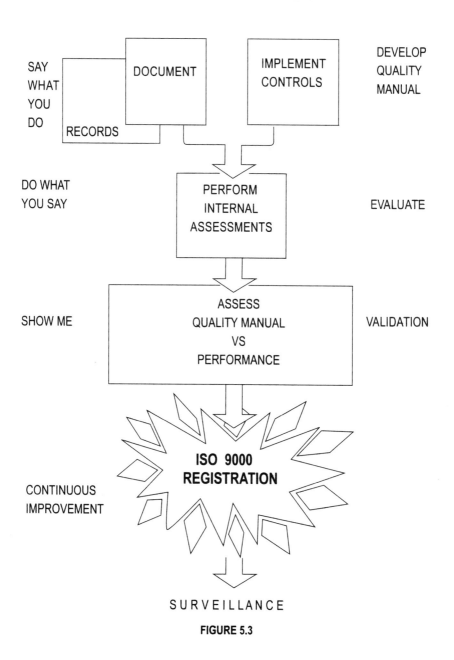

FIGURE 5.3

Being able to successfully demonstrate that everyone in your organization is "doing what they say they are doing," will lead to an ISO 9000 registration and the subsequent issuance of an ISO 9000 certificate. The final and eternal aspect of ISO 9000 is the formal surveillance audit (conducted two to three times a year). Here, the company will again be visited by the external (third party) assessors in order to prove that the company is still doing what it says it is doing. As the company continue to grow, adapt to new business situations, take on new responsibilities, stop doing other things, etc. it is important that the quality system continues to reflect the company's commitment. A successful ISO 9000-compliant organization will "continuously improve" its quality operations.

6 THE DECISION TO IMPLEMENT

Emphasis on quality should always be an integral part of your company's philosophy. As new quality-oriented insights appear, a dynamic organization will incorporate these concepts and utilize them to improve its operations.

Understanding the nature and scope of the ISO 9000 standards is fundamental and will often lead an organization to consider implementation. Careful interpretation and analysis of worldwide business conditions indicates that the pursuit of an ISO 9000 registration is both logical and sensible. Keep in mind that you should perceive ISO 9000 as an opportunity, not as another regulatory threat.

One of the best ways to get started is through a staged or phased approach. Begin small and build on your successes.

The answers to the following set of questions will influence where and how to initiate the ISO 9000 journey:

1. Does the existing quality-oriented system within the group, function or organization have clear and understandable rules and procedures in place?

2. Will seeking an ISO 9000 registration provide an achievable set of goals?

3. Can attainment of these goals be measured in some meaningful way, such as improved cost structures, reductions of waste, better customer perceptions, etc.?

As an example, it is best to implement ISO 9000 through a managed and phased approach by solidifying senior management's commitment to the program, establishing a set strategy and purpose, and utilizing a team of dedicated and resourceful people (Figure 6.1).

IMPLEMENTATION STRATEGY

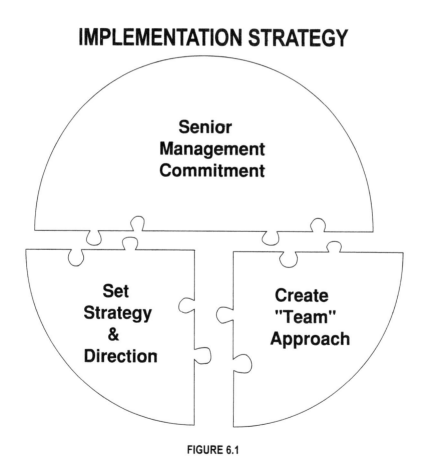

FIGURE 6.1

Having established an overall company perspective, the actual ISO 9000 implementation is left up to the individual business unit/ organizational entity. Each unit should be empowered to define its own needs and requirements and to develop a customized implementation approach (schedule, responsibilities, teams, tools to use, focus and incentives). This is not as formidable as it appears, since the early experiences with ISO 9000 have provided a great deal of insight and information on how to successfully navigate this quality journey.

KEY TO SUCCESS

The fundamental reason for the success enjoyed by the various groups in their pursuit of ISO 9000 can be attributed to one factor: the WILLINGNESS TO SHARE! The early pioneers were able to communicate their successes as well as their failures. In fact, more was learned from the mistakes and how to avoid them. The ISO 9000 experience has proven to be unique by fostering communication and instilling a willingness to share across communities throughout most companies.

A company can capitalize on the sharing phenomenon by channelling this effort through a number of formalized mechanisms. For example, one way to accomplish this is through the establishment of discipline-specific councils, where each of the respective groups meets on a regularly scheduled basis and creates strategy, directions, goals, roles, responsibilities. Additionally, these councils provide a forum for disseminating "experiences" on behalf of their respective communities.

If you are dealing with a large number of sites, consider developing a system for transmitting ISO 9000- related information throughout the company in order to allow all of your potential registrants to stay abreast of the current findings. This will not only serve to facilitate individual ISO 9000 programs in your various locations, but will prevent the widespread occurrence and duplication of errors and provide a vehicle for early warning alerts. As an example, Appendix 14 illustrates an on-line information sharing network which was created to link a large, multinational company's various sites.

However, if you have a medium or small organization, then strive to get everyone involved at the same time. This will expedite matters and create an "esprit de corps."

In trying to decide whether to implement or how best to accomplish an ISO 9000 program, keep in mind the fundamentals of what will be needed. Basically you will require the following:

1. PEOPLE   (who are...)
    AUTHORIZED
    COMPETENT
    ORGANIZED
    RESPONSIBLE

2. PROCESSES   (which are...)
    CONSISTENT
    REPEATABLE
    TRACEABLE
    VISIBLE

3. FOCUS - FOCUS - FOCUS - FOCUS - FOCUS

ISO 9000 represents an international quality standard voluntarily adopted by over 80 countries, worldwide. ISO 9000 enjoys the largest amount of global recognition of any program of its nature. On the negative side, concerns persist that this program is fraught with domination, coercion, and deception in its claims. The truth probably lies somewhere between the two. There is little question that this quality effort has caught on around the world, as evidenced by the phenomenal growth of registrations (approaching 90,000, with no end in sight). In the U.S. alone, registrations have grown from a little over 200 in the first quarter of 1992 to approximately 5,500+ by year-end 1994. Current projections have estimated over 30,000 companies actively considering registration for their sites.

Anyone who has dealt with the standards knows the guidelines and wordings are often vague, obtuse and confusing. This has led to speculation that only a select few can understand and interpret the standards —those who actually create and modify them (registrars and industry consultants). The charge is that there is a self perpetuating society in the quality game for their own profit-oriented motives.

Whether this is true or not remains to be seen, and the hope is that this charge is only conjecture, and not fact. Given that the potential for deception and abuse can exist, the following guidelines should always be considered when embarking on an ISO 9000 journey:

1.   MAKE SURE YOU UNDERSTAND WHY YOU ARE
      SEEKING ISO 9000

2.   STAY IN CONTROL OF THE OVERALL PROCESS

      *   ISO 9000 is one small step in the TQM equation
      *   No one but you should have control of the quality management system. This is not something that can be developed by the quality department and then distributed. Everyone must be involved!

3.   MANAGEMENT INVOLVEMENT IS ABSOLUTELY
      ESSENTIAL

      *   Maintain a clear focus on your objectives and ensure success by obtaining an organizational commitment to make it happen. This clearly will require active involvement and utilization of a team concept.

4.   PREPARATION PROCESS IS KEY

      *   Understand all of the requirements

* Take the time to develop a "gap analysis" before you start (this will provide a good assessment of your current compliance capabilities and where the most obvious problems lie).
* Documentation will be the most difficult challenge, and you need to ensure that the proper or right amount is produced. Overdocumenting is as harmful as underdocumenting.
* The backbone of the ISO 9000 program is the INTERNAL AUDIT SYSTEM. It is the most important element of the entire program.

5.   WATCH COSTS!

* Plan, don't panic
* NEGOTIATE - NEGOTIATE - NEGOTIATE ... (for everything!)
* Learn from others (especially from their mistakes)
* ISO 9000 is becoming big business and, as is often the case, those who tell you that quality should be expensive, earn a living from it.

6.   CAVEAT EMPTOR (Let the buyer beware)

Finally, having decided to go forward with an ISO 9000 implementation, be aware that this concept stands as much chance of being accepted as any other quality program your company may have chosen to pursue in the past. It will be rare that ISO 9000 will be readily accepted by all your personnel (without some form of executive direction, pressure, coercion, explanation, rationale, etc.). Based on the number of previous attempts at introducing quality, an organization will face a series of "anti" arguments, all designed to explain why this program should NOT be done! Generally, the reasons for not doing quality (ISO 9000) will fall into one of the following categories:

I. PURPOSE

"We can't do ISO 9000 because our primary and all-consuming goal is to _____ "

1) make money
2) finish on time
3) bring our project in below cost targets
4) not impact our current schedules

II. CUSTOMERS

" We can't do ISO 9000 because _____ "

1) our audience is (your customer set) and they don't need it, or want it, or believe in it, etc.
2) we know more about the quality of our own products/ services than our customers do
3) we know what our customers want and we don't need ISO 9000 to tell us that
4) quality is not a major factor in our customer's decision to do business with us
5) our customers can't tell the difference anyway

III. PERFORMANCE

"We can't do ISO 9000 because _____ "

1) it costs more to provide this type of assurance and we won't recover the added expenditures
2) our successes generally arise from large, innovative gains. This is much too detailed and bureaucratic.
3) it will definitely cost too much and we will never be financially competitive
4) we don't have the time

IV. PEOPLE

"We can't do ISO 9000 because _____"

    1) our management philosophy believes and supports all quality efforts, but our present focus is clearly strategic and not aimed at the operational aspects outlined in this program

    2) our quality group has developed the current quality direction. We can't afford to have our people switched in midstream

    3) our work force is much too busy to take the time to document their processes

    4) we don't have processes in our company. We pretty much innovate as we need to

V. IMPROVEMENT

"We can't do ISO 9000 because _____"

    1) if it ain't broke, we don't fix it

    2) it really doesn't have anything to do with "continuous improvement" and we really believe that is the key

    3) our last attempts at implementing quality burned out after a few months, and we really didn't change anything, anyway

We've all heard these arguments and, in most cases, they represent an unwillingness to change and adapt to new ways of thinking. Do not be dissuaded. Acknowledge the argument for what it is and, assuming that you feel ISO 9000 is the right course of action for your company, begin to chart a course for implementation (Figure 6.2). (Also see Chapter 7, "How To Implement an ISO 9000 Program.")

ISO 9000 JOURNEY

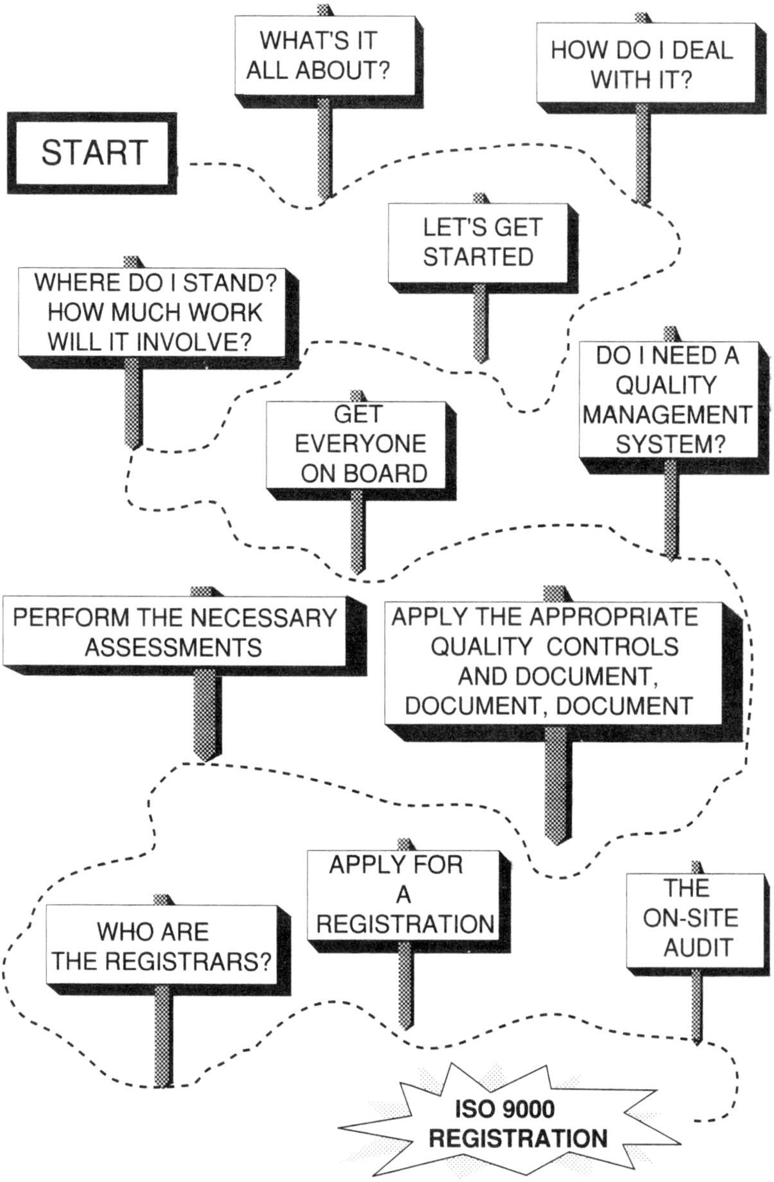

WHAT'S IT ALL ABOUT?

HOW DO I DEAL WITH IT?

START

LET'S GET STARTED

WHERE DO I STAND? HOW MUCH WORK WILL IT INVOLVE?

DO I NEED A QUALITY MANAGEMENT SYSTEM?

GET EVERYONE ON BOARD

PERFORM THE NECESSARY ASSESSMENTS

APPLY THE APPROPRIATE QUALITY CONTROLS AND DOCUMENT, DOCUMENT, DOCUMENT

APPLY FOR A REGISTRATION

THE ON-SITE AUDIT

WHO ARE THE REGISTRARS?

ISO 9000 REGISTRATION

FIGURE 6.2

Unfortunately, several obstacles remain that you will need to keep in focus as you move ahead. One of the more fascinating observations occurred in our sites AFTER we decided to pursue an ISO 9000 program. I have grouped these experiences into six "psychological stages," which just about every one of our locations appeared to encounter. (You may see similar reactions.)

PSYCHOLOGICAL STAGE I: DENIAL

Denial is the way most people deal with any form of new idea or, for that matter, change itself. "We don't need this, and besides it'll probably not have impact on the way I do things." Another reaction was to believe that if the program was ignored, then it would go away. "ISO 9000 is just that European thing and since I don't do business there, I don't need it."

In spite of this initial reaction, we continued to stress ISO 9000, and some of our sites moved to the next stage.

PSYCHOLOGICAL STAGE II: ANNOYANCE

Basically, "...get out of my face!" "ISO 9000 is just another one of a whole series of quality-oriented things that you people come up with to waste my time." Most organizations today have been bombarded with quality programs, innovations, suggestions, ideas, new concepts, etc. and the workers at the end of the chain cannot get too excited by the "quality program du jour." I have often heard that ISO 9000 is just today's program, and, therefore, why should anyone believe that this will be the true answer.

On the surface, the argument appears rational, however, this is not the case. Having experienced the first two reactions, do not be surprised by the appearance of stage III.

PSYCHOLOGICAL STAGE III: GRUDGING COMPLIANCE

This stage is often characterized by the decision makers shrugging their shoulders and saying, "Ok, fine, tell me what I have to do to pass this thing. What is the bare minimum we have to do in order to get a certificate?" This approach will be a terrible mistake if you allow it to prevail. ISO 9000 should NEVER be sought in order to merely obtain a certificate! This would be a waste of everyone's time and money. ISO 9000 will, perhaps for the first time, enable you to examine the fundamental aspects of how you operate and provide a vehicle for capturing the essence of your processes. Why waste this effort to only perform the minimum?

In some instances, management might say, "Ok, here's what we will do. We'll have the quality department spend some time developing a quality manual, and we'll make enough copies for everyone. Then we'll call in the registrars (auditors) and then we'll get a certificate and be done with this thing." Unfortunately, this will not work because the auditors are not stupid. Whom do you think they will audit - the quality department - who have just spent their time developing a "generic quality manual" or a "hypothetical quality system/manual?"

Not likely, the auditors are well aware that your company's quality department knows the quality system. No, the auditors will quickly determine that your people really cannot show that they are doing what they say (for one reason, they probably didn't say it in the first place—it was written by someone else). This approach will result in another waste of time, money, and effort.

There is no minimum, no quick and dirty way to address quality. It's possible that you might cleverly fool some of the auditors some of the time. You might even fool some of your customers —but not very likely. In essence, the only one you would be fooling would be yourself. And for what reason— in order to get a piece of paper saying you are compliant with the quality standards or have a quality system in place (when you really don't)? This charade is not the answer. Effort must be taken to avoid this trap and to move ahead.

We were able to detect this psychological stage and overcome the tendency to "minimize" the effort. Unfortunately, the next stage proved to be one of the most difficult.

PSYCHOLOGICAL STAGE IV: ROLLING UP THE SLEEVES

This is the work effort - full bore. It will take time, it will require commitment and it will take dedication. ISO 9000 doesn't happen unless **EVERYONE** makes it happen. That is both the negative and the positive aspect of the program and, as we've seen, it has rewards.

Once your organization is in the middle of an ISO 9000 program, you will shortly be exposed to the next, insidious stage. It generally appears late in the cycle, just before the visit from the external auditors.

PSYCHOLOGICAL STAGE V: STARK TERROR

This stage is characterized by the wholesale feeling of "I'll be the sole cause of our failure to pass the quality audit." The anxiety levels throughout your organization will be high, and people will begin to express unreasonable fears and exhibit strange behavior. You will notice an increase in absenteeism as the date for the "AUDIT" nears and optional vacation time will be taken. (The fear of failure can be quite nerve wracking).

All of these symptoms can be overcome through education, training, practice audits and generally preparing your people by reinforcing the notion that it is NOT they who are being audited, but the processes. Failure on an audit is never personal, and only through a concentrated effort can this fear be overcome.

Auditors are looking for evidence of a good quality system - one that reflects what the company is stating and in effect, doing. There is no need to panic. Most of the audits will be successful if you follow some basic rules: be prepared, answer factually and concisely, do not volunteer information, be aware that occasionally auditors might deliberately remain silent—people tend to feel uncomfortable with this silence and will often fill in the time with talk. If this happens, do not panic, but merely ask if the question had been answered or if the auditor needed anything more. Keep in mind that an external audit should never uncover anything in your system that you do not already know (this knowledge is generally gained through your own internal audit program). But if it does, an effective quality system will accommodate these nonconformances and be able to show that they will be handled in a logical and systematic fashion. Having successfully passed through the audit, your company is now faced with the final stage—one that may prove the most challenging.

PSYCHOLOGICAL STAGE VI: ACCEPTANCE AS THE WAY TO DO THINGS

A completely successful ISO 9000 program will eventually prove to be transparent to the way you operate. The idea is to integrate your quality system into the normal way you do business and not to focus on the specific elements of the ISO 9000 standard. Remember, ISO 9000 is not the end of the journey — it is only the first step on the road to quality. Organizations that have successfully achieved compliance with the standards have often reported that the registrars' surveillance visits are nonevents. The quality system is in place and operational and the assurance visits do nothing more than note that your system is up and running, per the stated objectives. Ensuring that these quality gains are not lost may be the most pressing issue you have to face.

7 HOW TO IMPLEMENT AN ISO 9000 PROGRAM

Countless books, publications, and articles deal with the best way to implement ISO 9000. However, let me say at the outset that there is no easy way to do it. It will take a tremendous dedication, commitment and effort on your part to make it happen. But, that is the rewarding aspect - the culmination of your activities will make it all worthwhile.

This chapter will outline a way to implement ISO 9000 throughout your various facilities. It represents the cumulative knowledge and experience of thousands of hardworking people, their successes and failures and the summation of their quality-oriented experiences. Unfortunately, a successful ISO 9000 program cannot be achieved through a series of shortcuts or "fill in the blank" aids. It requires a concentrated focus on the fundamental aspects of your operations and a willingness to examine these procedures in new and different ways. In most cases, you probably have sufficient processes in place, and they will stand the rigors of the assessment examination. For the operations that are less than definitive, an effort will have to be undertaken which will formalize the procedures and allow them to be documented and followed. How then to begin?

Although most functions profess to have processes in place or, at a minimum, a set of procedures which reflect the organization's efforts; one quickly learns that most of these systems are either lacking in documentation or poorly defined. In many instances, the processes are not being followed and there are substantial gaps between the documented procedures and practices.

The realization that these deficiencies exist, coupled with a desire to rectify the situation through ISO 9000 efforts is the initial step in the process. To be successful, five key factors must be employed (Figure 7.1).

FIRST STEP

FIRST, MANAGEMENT COMMITMENT IS ABSOLUTELY ESSENTIAL! There is no question that any effort of this magnitude requires management's dedication and backing. One of the best ways to induce this participation is to actively involve them from the beginning. Management will be called upon during the assessments, and a good practice is to schedule one or more preliminary audits of management's roles and responsibilities.

SECOND STEP

The second factor is to assign ISO 9000 implementation to a key member of the management team. This champion, along with an appropriate number of teams, can serve as the focal point and driving force behind the efforts. The actual number of teams and drivers will vary by function, but their focus is similar.

ISO 9000

KEY SUCCESS FACTORS

MANAGEMENT COMMITMENT

EDUCATION

ASSIGNED RESPONSIBILITIES

ISO 9000 REGISTRATION

AUDIT PROCESS

DOCUMENTATION SYSTEM

FIGURE 7.1

THIRD STEP

The third major ingredient is education. The ISO 9000 program must be communicated to each and every individual in the organization. As opposed to many other quality programs, ISO 9000 is a bottoms-up approach and will absolutely involve everyone! The education should provide a general awareness of ISO 9000, what it is, how it's accomplished, why it's being done, etc., and should also cover specifics for designated groups or individuals; either per project or per location. In this way, the seeds of everyone's role and contribution are planted and the roll-out can be efficiently accomplished.

DOCUMENTATION ADVICE

I KEEP SIX HONEST SERVING MEN

THEY TAUGHT ME ALL I KNEW

THEIR NAMES ARE WHAT AND WHY AND

WHEN AND HOW AND WHERE AND WHO

THE ELEPHANT'S CHILD
RUDYARD KIPLING

FIGURE 7.2

FOURTH STEP

The fourth key factor is the act of documentation. One of the mainstays of the ISO 9000 program is the act of documenting the functions' processes in a way that is meaningful and reflects what is going on. One of the best ways to start is by using the advice found in Rudyard Kipling's, The Elephant's Child (Figure 7.2). Simply concentrate on what is being done, why you do certain things, when events occur, under what circumstances, how tasks are accomplished, where controls apply and when; and throughout all of the various operations, who is responsible. The answers to these and similar questions will be the summation of your quality procedures. A more formal explanation can be found in Figure 7.3.

Your processes can be depicted in a variety of ways such as a checklist, a diagrammatic flowchart, or a list of development procedures. It does not matter as far as ISO 9000 is concerned. What matters is that you and your people are comfortable with these descriptions and that they reflect what actually is going on in your operations. The processes are driven by a set of requirements (things that the department or function are given or are being asked to provide). Almost all processes have dependencies on others, and these should be noted. Finally, the results of the department's efforts are known as outputs; fundamentally, the reason the group is in existence. The net result is the documentation of all of your quality processes, or what is known as a quality manual.

When preparing your documentation, it is advisable that your procedures be organized both correctly and in a logical order. Clearly, the documentation itself must be legible as well as easy to understand and follow. Finally, do not overlook grammar and spelling. If you are going to do something, do it right the first time!

The documentation should take the form of a quality manual which contains all of the relevant procedures and work instructions which have a direct impact on the quality processes. Overall, a quality manual must encompass the general high level quality policies, procedures and practices of an organization, as well as certain specific areas such as purpose, objectives, scope, mission (it's best to in-

FUNCTIONAL PROCESS

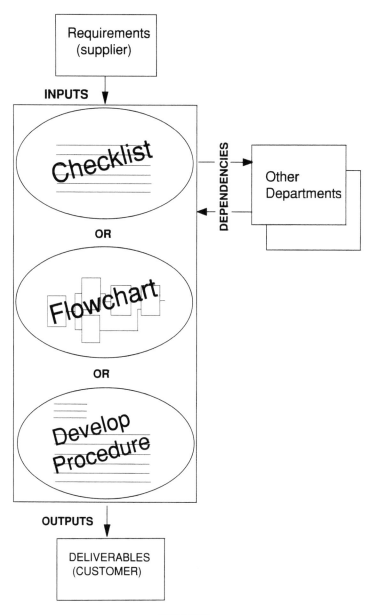

FIGURE 7.3

clude business flow diagrams), organization charts (delineating senior management responsibilities), details of the quality organization,
policy statements reflecting compliance with the various ISO 9000
elements (the 20 clauses of ISO 9001), appropriate terms and definitions, the distribution list for the quality manual, the control process
for the quality manual and various references (such as corporate/
execution instructions, edicts, directives, etc.).

One of the more useful techniques is use of "Department Operating Manuals" or "DOM's." Fundamentally, these DOM's allow
groups to formally record and periodically review all the operational
activities of a department and focus on the controls which are used to
assure that the various operations are being effectively managed.
DOM's typically contain ten elements:

1. MISSION

What is the basic business of the group? Identify the key
objectives and the main goals and outline the criteria for
achieving success.

2. STRATEGY

Indicate how the department will achieve the goals outlined
in the "Mission." Basically, how is the department going to get
where it plans on going? Identify the various activities, the
responsibilities, what is required, the boundaries of responsibility
and which subprocesses are required to be employed.

3. DEPENDENCIES

Which organizations provide support and/or requirements and
who does the department rely on for information, etc. This section should include an identification of specific departmental
customers, suppliers, and associates, as well as spell out the key
interfaces, the critical success factors, and any training or education that might be necessary.

4. DELIVERABLES

What does the department produce (another way of noting the outputs)? Identify requirements, any inter-company agreements, consigned materials, handling and storage of various materials, etc. If the department in question is a service provider, there is a need to delve into the extent of this service as well as the frequency; also indicate the exceptions.

5. PROCEDURES

In effect, how do the people within the department know what to do? Focus on specific work instructions and operating practices. This might also include such items as user guides, procedural flow charts, scheduling algorithms, checkpoints and control over all documented areas.

6. MANAGEMENT CONTROL SYSTEM

How does the department know if it is performing correctly and IF NOT, what would they do about it? Indicate the various process measurements, reports, significant indicators, customer satisfaction indices, statistical quality control elements, results of inspection or validation techniques, or meeting notes (minutes). Discuss what is done with nonconforming products and how unaccountable variations are controlled. Ensure an underlying base of records retention.

7. CHANGE MANAGEMENT

How and when does the department handle change? Measure the changes in requirements, the frequency, the responsiveness of the department to react to the called-for changes, how unexpected change is handled, which corrective actions are employed and when and how the department removes obsolete items. Make sure the documentation reflects the latest innovations and communication across all departmental members.

8. IMPROVEMENTS

What is the department doing to make things better? This question should involve analysis and simplification techniques, the use of any quality improvement teams and techniques, use of defect elimination criteria, reduction in cycle time, waste elimination, and productivity gains. Comment on whether these measures are affordable, and generally attempt to develop a best-of-breed philosophy.

9. QUALITY RECORDS

Which records are maintained, and how does the department assure that these records support and validate the various quality approaches? Some of the information includes the results of intradepartmental audits and calibration of tools, as well as various desk procedures.

10. UPDATE AUTHORIZATION

Basically, who is authorized to update the DOM? When and why? Supporting this area are specifics aimed at key names and responsibilities.

Conceptually, documentation should take a four-tiered approach (Figure 7.4), where the top tier is the organization's policy and objectives (for each of the various ISO 9000 programs). The second tier is aimed at actual operating procedures (within a department group, or through a team) containing information such as who is responsible, what is done, when is it accomplished, what are the various interfaces and where is the effort concentrated. The third tier deals with various work instructions (how does one do the job) and provides details on the performance of specific tasks. The fourth tier contains the required quality records (forms, books, files, etc.) which address the auditor's requirement to verify the actions (these are generally the answers to the "Show Me" questions). Several organizations have utilized this approach and have even gone to using different colored paper to reflect the various tiers.

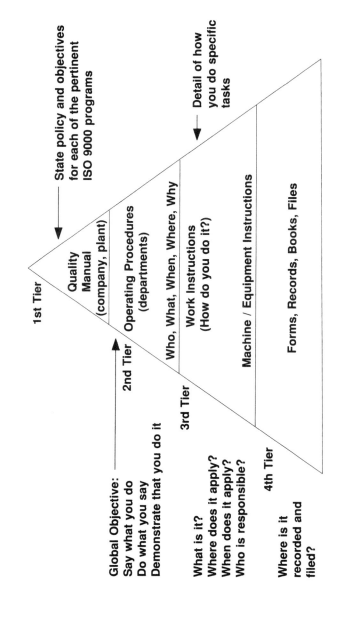

THE DOCUMENTATION PYRAMID

1st Tier

Quality Manual (company, plant)
— State policy and objectives for each of the pertinent ISO 9000 programs

2nd Tier

Operating Procedures (departments)
Who, What, When, Where, Why

3rd Tier

Work Instructions (How do you do it?)
— Detail of how you do specific tasks

Machine / Equipment Instructions

4th Tier

Forms, Records, Books, Files

Global Objective:
Say what you do
Do what you say
Demonstrate that you do it

What is it?
Where does it apply?
When does it apply?
Who is responsible?

Where is it recorded and filed?

FIGURE 7.4

94

Many registered sites have taken the approach of using on-line documentation in meeting the requirements of ISO 9000. This is clearly acceptable under the guidelines and, in many cases, is the preferred way to demonstrate adequate control principles. There are several distinct advantages to maintaining on-line documentation, and they include:

1. Maintaining accuracy by allowing for on-line reviews of any proposed changes, as well as maintaining a history file which can illustrate the date and nature of the changes

2. Ensuring controlled access and providing capabilities for appropriateness and security of those individuals empowered to perform modifications

3. Allowing easier and highlighted reviews, approvals, and changes.

4. Ensuring that all required information is complete before the issuance of a document, through the use of on-line checking features

5. Permitting immediate removal of any obsolete information, as well as providing a simultaneous start-up date for the initiation of a given document.

In order to provide a single, consolidated view for the control of the quality manual, many organizations elect to implement a quality management system (Figure 7.5). This system is completely optional and is not required for ISO 9000. A typical "quality management system" consists of an on-line, software documentation system which is used to assist in the overall management of an organization's quality records and operational procedures. It acts as the single repository for all of the information required for demonstrating compliance to ISO 9000.

QUALITY MANAGEMENT SYSTEM

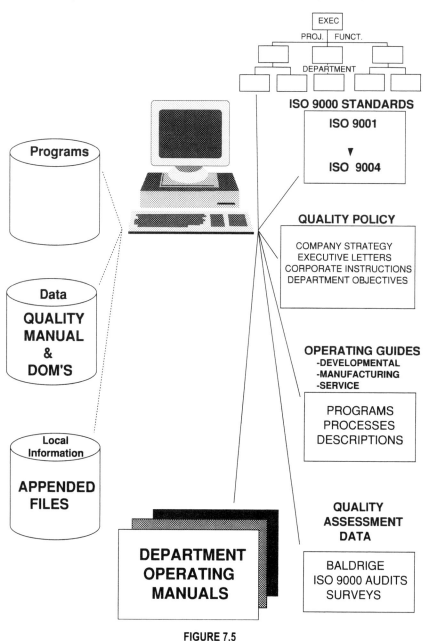

FIGURE 7.5

Generally speaking, a quality management system contains the aforementioned quality manual, the various DOM's (Department Operating Manuals), organization charts, linkages to various division and corporate operating procedures, the ISO 9000 standards (for reference purposes), an ability to provide on-line, real-time data entry capabilities as well as provisions for hard-copies (normally restricted to day-of-use). The use of the on-line capability not only makes life easier for everyone at a site, but it gives one the benefit of controlling the documentation by ensuring that only the on-line version represents the official documentation and any hard copies are automatically noted as "working copies only." One of the primary documentation problems is to ensure that people know the quality manual is in effect "and current." Companies will define the on-line version in that regard and everything else is defined as "not-official."

FIFTH STEP

The fifth major factor is the implementation of a "quality audit process." This process is essentially a plan for assessing a function's stated quality management system compared with the required elements of the ISO 9000 standard; then comparing the quality management system to what is actually being done by the respective groups in the organization.

The quality assessment process should contain a plan for each of the major groups or teams, an evaluation of the training requirements and level of knowledge, an optional series of self-assessment tools (e.g., questionnaires), and the results of the various audits which reflect the comparison of "Do What You Say" and "Prove It."

Several types of audits can be performed: internal self audits, internal (peer) audits, internal (pre-assessment) audits, external (pre-assessment) audits conducted by employees which are not part of the specific function; and external (pre-assessment) audits conducted by the third-party registrars. The actual registration audit is always conducted by the third-party auditor/registrar.

One of the ways an organization reduces the cost of ISO 9000 is through the use of "internal auditors." These are your own employees, specifically trained to conduct ISO 9000 assessments. Once these people are trained and exposed to ISO 9000, the validity of their findings should correlate highly with the findings of the external auditors. In fact, in the majority of situations, your own auditors are more stringent (since they presumably know where to look and which of the various procedures are most likely to give a site trouble). Through the extensive use of this resource, you should be able to identify and solve numerous problems BEFORE calling in the external or third-party assessors.

The Registration Assessment involves the registrar's on-site audit of a location's operations. This evaluation compares the actual implementation of the quality system to the documented accounts. In addition, the registrar's assessment determines whether or not a quality process fulfills the minimum requirements established in the ISO 9000 standard.

Some registrars may first suggest that they conduct a high level pre-assessment. A pre-assessment will help determine whether or not a quality program is ready for ISO 9000 registration. This first-pass approach will uncover many problem areas which might be caused by misunderstanding or misinterpreting the standards. Since it's billed as a preliminary investigation, the atmosphere is less threatening than a formal (Pass-Fail) audit and enables the "auditee" to understand where major problems reside. The auditor will also use this time to learn more about the area in question.

At best, an audit is a random selection of clauses and/or people to ascertain whether an organization substantially complies with the ISO 9000 standards. It is based on the assumption that the audit is not a one-time event, but an integral part of a total evaluation scheme; consisting of self audits, peer reviews, and a regularly scheduled pattern of visits by the registrar (surveillance audits). It should always be noted that the main effort (and realized benefit) is always INTERNAL to the company being audited. An auditor will not only observe what is going on, but will generally ask a series of questions (Figure 7.6) designed to elicit responses indicating that you are doing what you say you are doing. In almost every instance, the auditor will ask for demonstrable proof, often by using the expression, "Show Me."

TYPICAL ASSESSMENT (AUDIT) QUESTIONS

WHAT DO YOU DO ?

WHERE IS THAT DEFINED ?

WHY DO YOU DO THIS ?

HOW DO YOU REVIEW IT ?

ARE REVIEWS FORMAL OR AD-HOC ?

WHO DO YOU REPORT THIS TO ?

HOW DO YOU MEASURE IT ?

DO YOU TRACK PROBLEMS ?

DO YOU TRACK CORRECTIVE ACTIONS ?

DO YOU CONDUCT AUDITS AGAINST ISO 9000 REQUIREMENTS ?

DO YOU HAVE PROCEDURES ?

DO PROCEDURES REFLECT THE CURRENT PROCESS ?

DO PROCEDURES REFLECT ALL OF THE PROCESSES ?

WHERE IS THIS OPERATION MENTIONED ?

DO YOU HAVE A TRAINING PROGRAM ?

ARE ALL MEMBERS OF THE DEPARTMENT INCLUDED ?

DO YOU KEEP RECORDS OF TRAINING ?

HAVE YOU RETAINED YOUR QUALITY RECORDS ?

WHAT IS THIS FORM FOR ?

DOES THIS FORM HAVE A FORM NUMBER ?

ARE RETENTION PERIODS FOR RECORDS SET ?

•

THE OVERALL KEY IS "SHOW ME"!

FIGURE 7.6

One of the most important aspects of the entire ISO 9000 registration process is preparing the site or location for the external audit. This preparation is vital to the overall success and must be carried out with the same level of intensity as ensuring that the appropriate quality processes are established, well documented, understood and in practice.

Prior to the external auditor's on-site visit, the following guidelines should be established and in place:

1. The entire management team must understand the complete registration process, including the audit itself. (The actual audit is a visit by a group of impartial, objective assessors whose purpose is to verify that the area is in compliance with a set of international standards.) The auditors' training and experience is directed toward obtaining factual support of the documented processes.

2. The auditors should not place you on the defensive, nor for that matter should people become protective. It really isn't necessary to hide, confuse or obscure information. Basically, the auditors are attempting to verify that what you have stated is, in fact, what you are doing.

3. The auditors are governed by the guidelines found in the ISO 10000 series which outline the structure, conduct, training and management of the actual audit. The ISO 10000 standards delineate the responsibilities of the auditor, as well as those of the auditee. (It is therefore prudent for the ISO 9000 applicant to become familiar with the ISO 10000 standards and understand the nature and possible impact on their particular site). For example, responsibilities of the auditee will include telling the relevant employees about the objectives and scope of the audit; appointing responsible members of the staff to accompany members of the audit team; providing all the resources needed by the audit team (one practical suggestion is to meet with the audit team in their hotel prior

to the actual visit and provide them with maps, organization charts, directions, logistics, etc. which help establish a healthy environment and one which is conducive to a good working relationship); providing access to the facilities and evidential material; maintaining a cooperative attitude which will prove mutually beneficial; working in a positive way toward the corrective actions based on the audit findings (this is one of the major audit areas and the auditors are especially keen on seeing prompt and effective responses to the identified nonconformances).

4. Explaining the overall process to everyone at the location will go a long way toward reducing anxiety and helping things go smoothly. Items which should be highlighted include: ensuring that everyone has the correct documentation; emphasizing it is the system (process) that is being audited (and not the people); and focusing on honest and correct responses to auditor questions as the best way to respond.

5. The key is constant vigilance by everyone, which will ensure an ongoing pattern of successes and progress. Key to this equation is management's active participation and unwavering commitment to the quality objectives being pursued. Combined, these factors will allow an organization to build on any ISO 9000 success and make quality a normal part of the operation.

COMMON ASSESSMENT DEFICIENCIES

Based on experiences with the ISO 9000 program, the following is a list of typical deficiencies which have occurred during preliminary and final audits (Figure 7.7). This list should merely serve as a sentinel for any of your future ISO 9000 assessment efforts. Keep in mind that this list is not all-inclusive, but highlights the most frequent areas of concern:

1. Documentation
   - Unapproved levels
   - Procedures do not match practices
   - Unofficial changes
   - Obsolete versions in use
   - Not located per stated distribution
   - Incomplete records/poor filing system

2. Products/Materials
   - Unapproved material
   - Improper handling and storage
   - Inadequate shelf life
   - Quality status not clearly indicated
   - Inadequate control of nonconforming material
   - Extensive use of "use as is" disposition
   - Nonconformances not identified
   - Packaging not adequate to protect quality

3. Training
   - Inadequate training
   - Lack of awareness of requirements
   - Noncompliance with existing procedures
   - Responsibilities not defined and understood

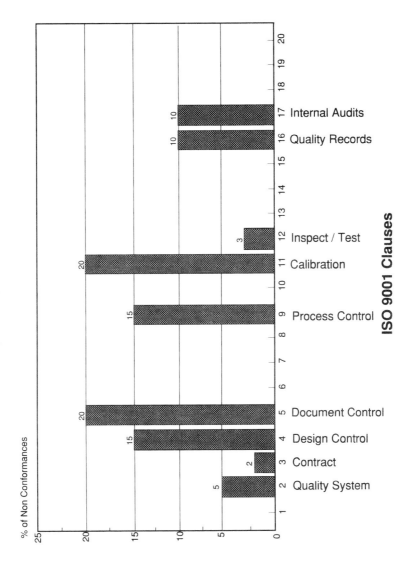

FIGURE 7.7

4. Calibration
- Calibration schedules not adhered to
- Measurement standards not calibrated
- Procedures lacking for assessing disposition of already tested products found to be out of calibration

5. Corrective Actions
- Not determined
- Not documented
- Too slow
- Not fully implemented
- Actions not adequately verified

The fundamental key to an effective ISO 9000 implementation is the ability to share information and disseminate the findings across your organization in a meaningful way. In addition to establishing an environment conducive to sharing, we created and developed an entire battery of tools and aids which assisted in all of our ISO 9000 efforts. Many of these support-type products dealt with the enormous task of controlling the documentation and (like the Quality Management System described above), they were all designed to enhance and embellish our on-line approach. By providing a seamless environment, we were able to accommodate the rigors of ISO 9000 in such a way that our employees felt it was part of their normal environment. This is essential, and you should strive to accomplish ISO 9000 within the framework of how you normally operate. Remember, it is not necessary to develop an on-line capability—especially if you are not already there; nor for that matter should you try to introduce any other new concepts while seeking ISO 9000. Try to install ISO 9000 as seamlessly as possible. ISO 9000 is completely flexible and will accommodate just about any variety of implementation mechanics.

All of the ISO 9000 techniques (sharing, utilizing tools and aids and developing best-of-breed procedures), were built on four guiding principles: (1) Management Commitment (2) Education (3) Participation and (4) Communication. This is the formula for success (Figure 7.8).

FUNDAMENTAL TECHNIQUES

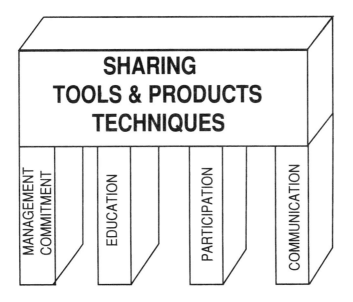

FIGURE 7.8

8 REGISTRARS and CONSULTANTS

The ISO 9000 standards were developed for use in contractual situations (such as those that exist between a supplier and a customer). There are provisions within the application of the ISO 9000 standard for self-audits (first party), and of course, the customer (second party) can always request an audit of your operation—as a condition of doing business. Obviously, whether the supplier agrees depends on the business situation.

The ISO 9000 standards go beyond this requirement by establishing the need for independent, impartial auditors (registrars). Their name comes from the fact that following an audit, a successful ISO 9000 applicant will be registered as having demonstrated compliance with the standards. (see Appendix 10 for a discussion of the difference between the terms "certification" and "registration").

Through the use of the independent auditors who have, themselves, complied with the required ISO 10000 series of standards, customers around the world can be assured that the ISO 9000 registration of a company or supplier in question has been performed in a uniform and standardized fashion. (Figure 8.1)

ISO 1000 SERIES

ISO 10011-1 AUDITING
PRINCIPLES
    -SCOPE, DEFINITIONS, OBJECTIVES
ROLES & RESPONSIBILITIES
AUDIT
    - PREPARATION, ASSIGNMENTS, DOCUMENTATION
CORRECTIVE ACTION FOLLOW UP

ISO 10011-2 QUALIFICATION CRITERIA FOR AUDITORS
PRINCIPLES
    - SCOPE, DEFINITIONS
EDUCATION, TRAINING
CODE OF CONDUCT

ISO 10011-3 MANAGEMENT OF AUDIT PROGRAMS
PRINCIPLES
MANAGEMENT PRACTICES
CODE OF ETHICS

FIGURE 8.1

ACCREDITATION BODIES AND REGISTRARS

With the exception of certain regulated products, the customer ultimately establishes the requirements for ISO 9000 conformance. The
degree to which registration is demanded may also be negotiable.
Obviously, at one extreme, a supplier stating a policy of conformance
may be sufficient; however, at the other end of the spectrum, buyers
may insist on ISO 9000 registration from a third-party firm or registrar which is accredited by one or more governmental organizations
known as "Accreditation Boards" (Figure 8.2).

TYPICAL "COUNTRY" STRUCTURE

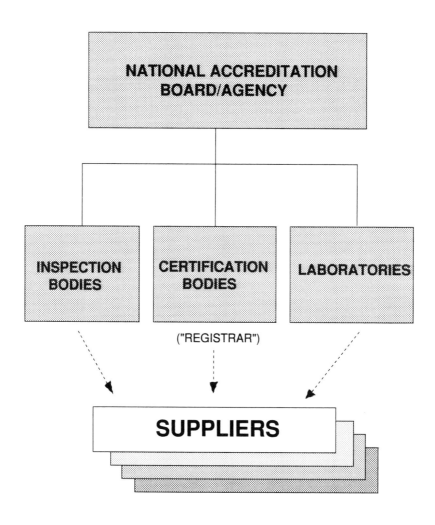

FIGURE 8.2

Accreditation bodies are those entities within a country that officially grant approval to registrars; registrars, in turn, perform audits (assessments) on companies seeking ISO 9000 registration (compliance). Some of the accreditation bodies in Europe are UK - NACCB (National Accreditation Council of Certification Bodies); Netherlands - RvC (Raad voor de Certificatie); Germany - TGA (German Accreditation Board). In the U.S., the accreditation body is called ANSI-RAB, which is the result of an agreement between the American National Standards Institute (ANSI)and the Registrar Accreditation Board (RAB); the latter a subsidiary of the American Society for Quality Control (ASQC). (Figure 8.3)

Today, there is no worldwide registrar recognition accreditation scheme in place. Unfortunately, this has led to a potpourri of recognition schemes ranging from "Memoranda of Understandings" between registrars; between registrars and a government; between registrars and accreditation bodies; as well as agreements that appear to be in place between governments themselves.

MUTUAL RECOGNITION OF ISO 9000
REGISTRATIONS

The International Organization for Standardization has created a group of worldwide experts to look at the problem of international recognition of quality systems registrations. The group is composed of representatives from various areas, e.g., suppliers of products and/ or services, customers of these suppliers, registration bodies, and accreditation bodies. The group is known as "QSAR" (Quality System Assessment Recognition), and they met for the first time in November 1993. Their mission is to develop a series of proposals which will finally solve the difficulties surrounding ISO 9000 registration acceptance. Given the degree of difficulty of the task, the compromises that will be required and the track record for speed in bringing agreed-to proposals forward, it is likely that an "ISO and IEC" (International Electrochemical Commission) endorsed plan will be years in the making.

ACCREDITATION AGENCIES

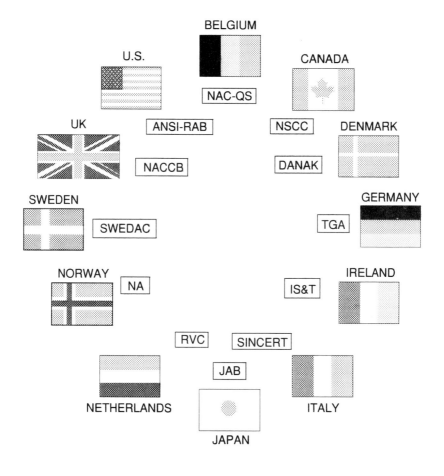

FIGURE 8.3

The current working proposal outlines a scheme for worldwide acceptance of ISO 9000 registrations—regardless of by whom or where the assessment is performed! (In essence, ISO 9000 certificates issued by U.S. registrars would carry the same weight in Europe as those issued by European registrars and, of course, vice versa).

In addition, the European Union is attempting to promulgate a standard for and harmonize recognition of government-sponsored accrediting bodies in Europe. (These are referred to as "notified" bodies). For example, registrations performed by NACCB accredited registrars in the UK would be recognized by notified bodies in the other countries in Europe (and vice versa).

Given this environment, it's more important than ever for companies to understand customer requirements. Since ISO 9000 is relatively new, and the number of ISO 9000-registered firms reasonably few, international customers have been slow to enforce the standard. To the extent that buyers include it in their purchase agreements, it is often done without specific reference to a particular level of ISO 9000 conformance. Similarly, accreditation is often left out of the requirement.

The best answer to the issue of recognition is that if an ISO 9000 registration is obtained from an accredited registrar (apparently regardless of the specific recognition), then (in theory) it will be recognized by others. So far, there has not been a conclusive test of this theory—one way or the other—but the indications are that any registrar's recognition is better than no recognition at all (see Appendix 5).

HOW TO CHOOSE A REGISTRAR

The following list of guidelines/attributes are the most significant to keep in mind when selecting an appropriate registrar:

1. Cooperative Attitude
2. Demeanor
3. Competence
4. Experience
5. Cost
6. Accreditation
7. Mutual Recognition
8. Conflict of Interest (although this is at the bottom of the list, an obvious conflict of interest will disqualify any ethical registrar. An applicant should not have to give much weight to this consideration).

I believe the two most important attributes are a cooperative attitude and demeanor. Remember, you will maintain a long-term relationship with the registrar, and it's extremely important that this relationship be agreeable. I do not mean to suggest that the registrar should be easy or should look the other way (any credible registrar should not allow that to happen); for both your sake and theirs they must protect their professional integrity at all cost).

Although competence is important, I have also found that registrars do not (and should not) be telling you anything that you don't already know. The backbone of the ISO 9000 program is centered around a complete and working internal audit program. If you are doing your job properly, you will uncover potential ISO 9000 deficiencies BEFORE the registration audit. Keep in mind, registrars NEVER "confer" any status (they don't have that power), but they do "confirm" that which you should already know! In reality, your own competence in recognizing where procedures are missing or out of control is much more important than having an external set of eyes uncovering your own problems. A third-party audit should never bring any surprises—thus competence, as an attribute, is not as key as the other aspects.

Costs are also down on my list, since the registrar's costs in seeking an ISO 9000 registration are generally a very small piece of the equation (most of the costs are associated with your own internal readiness and preparation). It's always important to identify all of the costs associated with an ISO 9000 registration, and most registrars will outline their cost structure for various items (e.g., audits, preassessments, desk checks, certificate fees, miscellaneous fees, and surveillance visits). It's also important to identify the lead time for an on-site visit. Currently, there is a huge demand for registrars' time, as more and more companies are seeking ISO 9000 registration. The registrars are often unable to service applicants due to their backlog, and this may be a factor in your selection.

ISO 9000 CONSULTANCY SERVICES

There may be several major reasons why a business about to embark on the ISO 9000 journey would choose to use a consultant. Clearly, an experienced ISO 9000 practitioner can assist in the overall project management as well as provide the appropriate technical expertise in terms of adapting the standards for the client in question. This assistance might take the form of interpretation of the standard or explaining the particular standard in terms of the client's business operations or practices. Developing and delivering the training and education programs will play a big part in the job, and care should be exercised in selecting the right amount of education (not too much and not too little) in order to get the client's personnel focused properly.

There is no substitute for practical experience! One of the most important ingredients an ISO 9000 consultant can bring is that they have actually been a part of an ISO 9000 registration (rather than merely talking about it). Experience will often allow clients to avoid costly mistakes and most certainly will reduce the learning curve—which will always prove to be a good investment.

Another facet of the operation is the applicant's assessment program (which is a mainstay of the ISO 9000 system). A good consultant will see that a solid, working program gets established and that the company maintains the appropriate documentation of its achievements (certainly to satisfy the auditors, but more importantly to satisfy the company itself).

Starting in 1992, the number of ISO 9000 consulting organizations increased dramatically, and the expectation is that this pace will continue. This huge expansion has flooded the market with all sorts of ISO 9000 consultants or advisors, many of whom have neither the expertise, experience nor time to include the kind of information a client requires; especially in terms of specifics relating to the client's industry or type of business.

The result is that most consultants are delivering the lowest common denominator, which often translates into generic lectures at exorbitant prices. In order to offset this trend, the following set of guidelines should be utilized by any potential client:

1. Ensure that the ISO 9000 standards/regulations are understood by the prospective consultant.

2. A consultant should have specific expertise in your industry and certainly expertise in the type of operation being performed (e.g., manufacturing, development, hardware or sofware being used, special solutions, unique services).

3. A consultant must have actual ISO 9000 experience—if the experience is limited to having attended a few classes or read some books, then the value of the advice is limited. With ISO 9000, there is no substitute for having gone through the preparation phase (including developing and documenting the processes, identifying the gaps, getting ready for "THE AUDIT," and living with the corrective actions.

4. A consultant must have familiarity with a number of registrars in order to help you select the appropriate registrar who is capable of conducting an audit (with the specifics of the client in mind). One of the most important aspects to this selection is the availability question. Due to the huge demand being placed on the registrars, it is not unusual to be subjected to a long waiting time. A good consultant should have first-hand experience with a variety of registrars and be in a position to share this knowledge accordingly. (Remember, all registrars are not alike!)

5. A consultant must be in a position to conduct and help conduct several pre-assessments on your behalf. Pre-assessments are of immense value. Quite often, consultants will tell a client "everything looks fine, and you will surely pass" only to have the registrar come in and find just the opposite. What a waste of time and money! Again, only people who have actually gone through an ISO 9000 process can appreciate this important point.

9 REGISTRATION RESULTS

Following a Final Assessment, a supplier can be Registered, Conditionally Registered, or Disapproved. Conditional Registration requires corrective actions, and the registrar will perform another on-site audit (generally referred to as a limited re-assessment) in order to ensure that corrective actions have been satisfactorily accomplished.

Successful ISO 9000 applicants receive a registration certificate from the registrar, along with a listing in the audit firm's directory. The suppliers are listed by "SIC" Codes (Standard Industrial Classifications). These SIC codes are used by the ISO 9000 registrars to denote the category in which to place an ISO 9000 compliant location or site. The registrars will publish the respective list of successful ISO 9000 applicants in their own manuals and periodically update these "buyer guides" as new sites are added or previously registered sites are dropped (no longer in compliance per the publishing registrar).

U.S. SIC codes and International ISIC codes are not the same. SIC codes are primarily used by the United States government to classify, categorize, and count activity within the economy. However, they are also used for analysis, marketing, organizational decisions, etc. Almost everything found in the media regarding the economy has underlying SIC codes.

As companies proceed toward ISO 9000 registration, it will become necessary to dialogue with the registrars in order to ensure that the company's function is properly placed within the registrar's list of compliant companies.

ISO 9000 certificates can expire, and the interval for expiration can vary from registrar to registrar. It is extremely important that one understand the limitations of the particular registration being offered. Moreover, even a valid ISO 9000 registration is always subjected to a periodic review (surveillance visits), by the registrar, approximately twice a year. Depending on the registrar, every two or three years, a complete reassessment is conducted.

Having successfully received an ISO 9000 registration, only a small number of ISO 9000 registrations are ever lost, and the main reasons appear to be as a result of mergers or facility closings. Generally, these events result in a change in personnel and/or direction. For a registered company to lose their registration/certification due to a breakdown in the quality system, the following would have to occur:

1. A major nonconformance is identified or a minor non-conformance is not addressed within an agreed-to, specified time period

2. The registered organization agrees to rectify the situation but deliberately does nothing (neglect)

3. The certificate is suspended by the registrar until the situation is remedied

4. The registrar cancels the ISO 9000 compliance because the situation is not rectified

Most registrars are very reluctant to take this extreme action. They would rather see the company maintain its emphasis on the quality system rather than exercise punitive measures.

Once a company receives notification that it has passed the final audit, it will be in a position to use the ISO 9000 notation in their advertising and associated literature. Keep in mind that one can use the fact that a company is ISO 9000 registered in all of its literature but cannot place this identification on any of its products!

The International Organization for Standardization has published guidelines for companies to follow in promoting their ISO 9000 registration. These guidelines are in the form of a 20-page brochure entitled "Publicizing Your ISO 9000 Registration." The brochure can be ordered from the country's representative to the International Organization for Standardization (see Appendix 4 for where to obtain ISO 9000 information).

Registrars also have guidelines for where and how to display the fact that they have found the applicant to be in compliance with the ISO 9000 standards. Unfortunately, along with many other areas surrounding ISO 9000, these guidelines are not uniformly agreed upon. Depending on the registrar chosen, the use of the registrar's logo (identification) as well as the stating of the ISO 9000 compliance will vary. Until the use is standardized, one should plan to use the registrar's specific guideline document to govern actions.

The best general advice on how to use the ISO 9000 notation is that it be used when there is a competitive advantage in the marketplace or when your audience knows and cares about it. This advantage will be temporary, and will go away when your competition is registered; therefore, it should be viewed as strictly a tactical move.

One suggestion regarding placement on an advertisement is to use the lower left corner but to tighten the "mice type" to avoid the spread of this information across the bottom of the page ("mice type" is the tiny, fine print at the bottom of print advertisements, often carrying disclaimers or legal terms and conditions). It is also recommended that the mice type be run UNDERNEATH the ISO 9000 mark.

Keep in mind the following "do's and don'ts" when referring to ISO 9000 in your advertising:

1. The International Organization for Standardization does not lend its name to advertisements, mainly due to the fact that they are NOT in the registration business, but are only responsible for creating and publishing international standards. (Use of their name or the notation "ISO" would imply that this organization has approved a certain registration or certification and according to the International Organization for Standardization, this usage would be false and misleading).

2. Be precise in advertising jargon, e.g., if a company only registered some of its locations, it would be wrong to state that the whole company is compliant.

3. Obviously, one cannot indicate that a product has been found compliant with the ISO 9000 standards.

4. Be careful with the word "accreditation" which has been incorrectly used in advertisements (the term "accreditation" is only used by accreditation agencies, not registrars).

5. Remember, ISO 9000 is not an award! To imply that one has won something by gaining ISO 9000 compliance is absolutely false and misleading!

6. Do not use any decal in your advertising unless there is a specific advantage. To be readable, a decal must be fairly large, but never larger than your company's logo. Remember that the ISO 9000 text must accompany any decal. Since most readers pick up only 2-3 messages per advertisement, the company's logo and message should always predominate.

7. Use the decal and text in product brochures, presentations, direct mail, newsletters, etc. It cannot be used in the product packaging e.g., box, containers. The ISO 9000 registration is for processes, not products. If it is misused, you can be forced to correct its usage—examples: reprint the packaging or issue a press release to correct a magazine article.

8. Do not use it on trinkets & trash. This only cheapens the significance of your achievement.

9. Make sure you inform all of your employees regarding the rules for using the decal/text. NOTE: improper usage could be grounds for decertifying a site. Decal usage is generally audited during the surveillance visits.

In the press, companies receiving an ISO 9000 registration are often referred to as "having achieved the 'highest' level of quality, as signified by the international award, etc." This is patently false! The three auditable standards (ISO 9001, ISO 9002, and ISO 9003) of the ISO 9000 series of quality standards are not meant to be a hierarchical ranking of achievement, but are merely ways to differentiate various business entities in seeking ISO 9000 compliance, based on what the company does. There is no real or implied gradation in receiving an ISO 9001 versus an ISO 9002 registration (it only notes that an ISO 9001 registrant included "Design Control" as part of their scope and the ISO 9002 registrant did not include this element).

HOW TO ANNOUNCE THAT YOU HAVE RECEIVED AN ISO 9000 CERTIFICATE

The following is a typical press release indicating an ISO 9000 registration:

PRESS RELEASE

Further information:
(Company contact)

COMPANY NAME (specific site/location etc) ·

MEETS ISO 9000 QUALITY STANDARD

(Date line)...__announced today that its ___(location/unit/site)

has met the ISO 9000 standard for quality assurance.

(Insert location/unit/site mission statement)
(Insert congratulatory quote from city/state/country government leader)
By complying with ISO 9000 requirements, _____ is maintaining its worldwide competitive position.

(Insert statement on location/unit export goods value or other trade activity).

"ISO 9000 is a set of international quality standards and guidelines for a quality assurance management system. It was established by the International Organization for Standardization and more than 80 countries have adopted it as a national standard. By year-end 1995, the number of U.S. registrations is expected to approach 10,000." (Insert executive quote from the company on the value of achieving the ISO 9000 registration, e.g., providing better product/service and what the value is for your customers. Emphasize the complementary aspects of ISO 9000 with your ongoing quality efforts and how the resultant combination of both quality programs will make your offerings that much better).

SCOPE OF THE ISO 9000 EFFORT

One of the truly unique aspects of ISO 9000 is that the quality standards do NOT apply to specific products. The ISO 9000 standards are generic in nature and are intended to enable a supplier to provide assurance that there is a quality system established and operational. The quality system will, in turn, allow the supplier to meet its stated quality objectives.

It is the quality system used to produce products and services that gets registered in compliance with the ISO 9000 standards (and not the end products or resulting services)!

As a result, an organization seeking ISO 9000 has a great deal of flexibility in deciding on the appropriate scope of the ISO 9000 registration. Individual product 'lines' or functional entities can be separately registered; or a single site can be registered; or a division with multiple sites/locations can be registered. In each of the cases cited above, a single certificate is issued for the defined scope.

There is no need to register all entities at one time. In many instances, it makes sense to have the various logical groupings seek registration and, as the organization gains experience and is able to transfer the required knowledge, additional functions can be added.

Some companies have two or more registered entities and will endeavor to combine these separate registrations under a single certificate of compliance. Other companies have everyone at a given location seek ISO 9000 registration (at the same time), basing this decision and action on the analysis that this is the most cost-effective and efficient approach for their particular set of quality-oriented processes. The bottom line is that any and all variations are acceptable, and it is up to the individual location or organization seeking ISO 9000 to determine what will work best for them.

How a company decides to publish its success with ISO 9000 is important, but even more so is what will the company (that achieves ISO 9000) actually do following that achievement?

> The dictionary defines "complacency" as: ...smug, self satisfaction, bovine, sluggish, dull... to be content to lose the desire to compete, to accept what is, instead of striving for what could be...

Unfortunately, many ISO 9000 registrants are seeing complacency creeping in their organizations once they have successfully achieved ISO 9000 registration. Although the dedication and work effort to obtain compliance is commendable and receipt of a certificate indicating the passing of an audit is worthy of admiration and praise, it is a fallacy to think that the journey to good quality has been accomplished. Quite the contrary!!! The journey has only just begun.

It is definitely a mistake to think that an ISO 9000 registration is the end-all; a mark of good quality to cherish forever. Those of you who follow the program and participate in its development will understand exactly what the registration means (nothing more and nothing less). Obtaining a successful registration should be an impetus to not only maintain the existing level of quality, but to use this progress to move forward! As more and more organizations begin to go through the surveillance phases of the ISO 9000 program, it is imperative that they not allow complacency to occur. It will be essential that you not lose the quality momentum initiated by the ISO 9000 effort. Ensure that the work performed to create and document the processes is carried on, and most importantly, do not rest on your laurels. In today's environment, one must continually strive to improve one's quality focus. It is essential for survival!

10 ISO 9000 AND TOTAL QUALITY MANAGEMENT

Many U.S. companies' approach to Total Quality Management (TQM) is patterned after the Malcolm Baldrige National Quality Award, using the format and philosophy inherent within this quality framework. The ultimate goal of these efforts is to maximize shareholder value by delighting customers with your products and services. This TQM philosophy is based on utilizing a set of efficient and effective approaches to operate a quality business.

ISO 9000, on the other hand, is a set of international quality standards which provide a foundation and complementary approach to your quality efforts by focusing on process documentation and maintaining suitable records. Your company's quality program will be able to build on this foundation by applying quality leadership principles, improving and re-engineering established processes, developing human resources, measuring progress, understanding your customers' expectations, and above all, doing whatever is necessary to ensure complete customer satisfaction.

The United States Malcolm Baldrige National Quality Award program contains elements which may be used as a criteria and standard against which organizations can measure their progress. As a diagnostic tool, it provides a common methodology for organizational self-examination resulting in the identification of areas of both strength and opportunity and leading to the development of an improvement plan. As a benchmark, it establishes the point from which all future progress can be measured.

The seven categories of the Baldrige criteria focus primarily on key areas of your business, including customer satisfaction and retention, market share and the strategy to improve it, leadership's role in driving the business, data and how it is used, product and service quality, productivity and operational effectiveness, human resource performance and development, and supplier performance and development. It examines the cause and effect relationship between methodology and results.

Utilizing these objectives, organizations describe their quality improvement system and expected outcomes. The Baldrige evaluation covers the breadth and depth of the organization's approach, deployment and results. The resulting strengths and opportunities for improvement provide organizations with a valuable perspective on their progress. Management can establish priorities by focusing resources on areas where opportunities for change and continuous improvement exist.

Although both ISO 9000 and Baldrige evaluate a company's quality achievement and utilize the services of trained, impartial evaluators to assess the respective level of attainment; the two are dramatically different in attitude, methodology, focus, utilization and applicability. By combining the best elements of both of these quality enhancing programs, you can create a concentrated and integrated approach which is aimed at identifying problems, developing creative and flexible solutions, and producing bottom-line benefits in your operations and processes.

Fundamentally, Baldrige asks for a description of your company's assurance processes and can best be summed up in the phrase "TELL ME." ISO 9000 requires the quality assurance processes to be documented, followed and proven. It can be summarized by the phrase "SHOW ME."

SEVEN CATEGORIES OF THE U.S. MALCOLM BALDRIGE NATIONAL QUALITY AWARD
(The relative statistical weighting is shown in parentheses See Figure 10.1)

1. LEADERSHIP (9%)

   The leadership of the organization is responsible for establishing the environment for excellence. This includes creating a customer orientation and focus throughout the organization. Clear and visible values, along with high expectations, must be generated. The leadership must be personally involved in planning, communications, review of plans/goals, and recognizing employees. They must also serve as role models and agents for change.

2. INFORMATION AND ANALYSIS (7.5%)

   Facts and data are required to support any business. Information needed to run the business must be identified, collected and analyzed. Information must be used for planning, setting objectives and priorities. Decisions should be based on facts.

3. STRATEGIC PLANNING (5.5%)

   Market leadership requires a company to focus on the future. Planning activities must determine or anticipate changes that will affect customer expectations. Strategic plans should be developed based on the drivers of customer satisfaction, customer retention and market share. The work environment must support the strategic environment or identify what must

1995 MALCOLM BALDRIGE SCORING VALUES

Point Values

1.0 Leadership   90

    1.1 Senior Executive Leadership..45

    1.2 Leadership System and Organization..25

    1.3 Public Responsibility and Corporate Citizenship...20

2.0 Information and Analysis   75

    2.1 Management of Information and Data.. 20

    2.2 Competitive Comparisons and Benchmarking 15

    2.3 Analysis and Use of Company-Level Data 40

3.0 Strategic Planning   55

    3.1 Strategy Development 35

    3.2 Strategy Deployment 20

4.0 Human Resource Development and Management   140

    4.1 Human Resource Planning and Evaluation 20

    4.2 High Performance Work Systems 45

    4.3 Employee Education, Training, and Development 50

    4.4 Employee Well-Being and Satisfaction 25

5.0 Process Management   140

    5.1 Design and Introduction of Products and Evaluation 40

    5.2 Process Management: Product and Service Production

        and Delivery 40

    5.3 Process Management: Support Services 30

    5.4 Management of Supplier Performance 30

6.0 Business Results   250

    6.1 Product and Service Quality Results 75

    6.2 Company Operational and Financial Results 130

    6.3 Supplier Performance Results 45

7.0 Customer Focus and Satisfaction   250

    7.1 Customer and Market Knowledge 30

    7.2 Customer Relationship Management 30

    7.3 Customer Satisfaction Determination 30

    7.4 Customer Satisfaction Results 100

    7.5 Customer Satisfaction Comparison 60

Total Points   **1000**

FIGURE 10.1

Source: U.S. Department of Commerce; Malcolm Baldrige National Quality Award

be done to ensure support. A key element of the long-range outlook is the development of employees, suppliers and business partners.

4. HUMAN RESOURCE DEVELOPMENT AND MANAGEMENT (14%)

The success of an organization depends upon the skills and motivation of a diverse work force. Human resource plans and practices must be developed in support of the overall business plan. To instill the right behaviors, there must be a synergistic relationship between hiring, performance evaluation, reward, recognition, and training. Employees should be well trained and empowered to make decisions.

5. PROCESS MANAGEMENT (14%)

Management must place emphasis on problem solving and waste prevention. A major issue in the environment is cycle time. Success in today's competitive markets demands ever shorter cycle times for new or improved products and services and more flexible responses to customers. Repeatable business processes must be aligned with the business strategy and continuously improved.

6. BUSINESS RESULTS (25%)

Real time measurements are necessary for the evaluation and improvement of the business and its processes. Measures of progress provide a results-oriented basis for channeling activities to deliver improved customer performance. Measurements should be developed from a customer view, not an internal view.

7. CUSTOMER FOCUS AND SATISFACTION (25%)

The success of a company will be determined by its customers. A customer-driven focus must address all stakeholders. Requirements and all aspects of the customer relationship must be understood. A method must be in place to gather, understand and act upon customer complaints. A method must exist to determine market segments and the requirements and expectations of these segments.

Companies' quality efforts are assessed against each one of the seven categories and a numerical score is determined based on the approach, deployment and results that have been achieved. The intent of the Malcolm Baldrige Award is to stimulate and motivate companies to new levels of quality and leadership through continuous improvement, excellence throughout, and prevention of errors. Correspondingly, ISO 9000 provides a customer with confidence in the suppliers' abilities to meet contractual demands through conformance to an established set of international standards, through control of the various quality processes that have been established in the organization, and a focus on both corrective and preventive actions.

Figure 10.2 illustrates a side-by-side comparison of the two quality-oriented programs. Some elements are unique to the Baldrige Award and likewise, some elements are unique to ISO 9000. A number of the quality aspects inherent in both programs have some relationship with each other (although it's fair to note that these relationships are not necessarily one-to-one). By mapping the degree of overlap between the two programs (Figure 10.3), it becomes apparent there is practically no ISO 9000 coverage in Baldrige category #6 "Business Results" and category #7 "Customer Focus and Satisfaction" (which constitute 50% of the Malcolm Baldrige Award scoring). On the other hand, ISO 9000 actually goes beyond the scope of a Baldrige examination in category #5 "Process Management," by concentrating on more areas and in pursuing these areas in greater depth.

The degree of overlap in the remaining four Baldrige categories is highly subjective and open to interpretation. The analysis indicates the approximate coverages as shown in the illustration. Keep in mind that neither program works to the detriment of the other and, in fact, their complementary natures can and should be used wherever possible.

Baldrige utilizes a methodology involving process description and, as mentioned previously, evaluation by a third-party. ISO 9000 encompasses the documentation of processes, including elaborate record keeping, and the verification that the quality process controls are being implemented and followed; which are also verified by the third-party audit process (Figure 10.4).

The Baldrige focus is heavily skewed toward customer satisfaction (25% of the weighting) and an equal emphasis is placed on achieving business results (25%). In contrast, ISO 9000 is more narrow in scope and mainly looks at the assurance of processes for producing goods and services through internal operations and responsibilities. There is practically no focus on customer satisfaction and very little emphasis for inclusion of business results. It is expected that these ISO 9000 deficiencies, customer satisfaction and business results, along with some relative measurements of value, will be addressed in the ISO 9000 Phase II revision cycle scheduled for the 1997 - 2000 time frame).

There are several other key differences: Baldrige is a voluntary program that is employed within the U.S. only. ISO 9000, on the other hand, can be required (generally as a condition of doing business) and is currently in existence in over 80 countries (eventually growing to 100 countries). Companies tend to embark on a Baldrige program as part of a corporate goal, and perhaps as a competitive response. Companies seeking an ISO 9000 registration will also do it for competitive reasons, but the corporate goal is minimized in light of governmental directives or contractual bid situations. Basically, you must be ISO 9000 registered to do business.

Finally, winning the Baldrige award is a competitive achievement; limited to a maximum of six companies in a given year (in three different categories: two in "large manufacturing," two in "small business" and two in the "service" categories). Having won the award, companies must wait a minimum of five years in order to re-apply. ISO 9000 is not an award, nor does it signify the total quality achievement of Baldrige. It represents the end result of a quality documenting and control process, which has been implemented, followed and verified by an auditor. There is no limit to the number of sites, locations, facilities, or companies. that can get registered (other than the limitations that the organizations may not be ready or the lack of sufficient, external assessors to perform the audits). Once a facility has achieved ISO 9000 registration, it must be re-evaluated on an average of every 6 months, forever! Depending on the registrar, an ISO 9000 registered site must be completely re-registered (evaluated) every two to three years. This constant and perpetual assessment indirectly mandates continuous improvement.

Many companies have found ISO 9000 to be a significant addition to a more robust implementation of a total quality management system. By combining the achievements of various (quality) industry leaders, the guidance of renowned quality consultants and the criteria as outlined in the United States Malcolm Baldrige National Quality Award, the European Foundation for Quality Management Award, the Shingo Prize, the Deming Award, etc. the result will be the creation of a necessary and sufficient set of activities, which when fully deployed and integrated, will yield world-class results.

COMPARISON OF BALDRIGE AND ISO 9000
-COMMON AREAS-

Baldrige Unique | Baldrige

1.0 LEADERSHIP
- ▶ 1.1 Senior Executive Leadership
- ▶ 1.2 Leadership System and
    1.3Public Responsibility & Corporate   Organization
    Citinzenship

2.0 INFORMATION & ANALYSIS
- ▶ 2.1 Management of Information
    2.2 Competitive Comparisons &   And Data
    Benchmarking
- ▶ 2.3 Analysis and Use of Company
       Level Data

3.0 STRATEGIC PLANNING

- ▶ 3.1 Strategy Development
    3.2 Strategy Deployment

4.0 HUMAN RESOURCE DEVELOPMENT &
    MANAGEMENT
    4.1Human Resource Planning & Evaluation
    4.2 High Performance Work Systems
- ▶ 4.3 Employee Education, Training
    4.4 Employee Well-Being & Satisfaction   & Development

5.0 PROCESS MANAGEMENT
- ▶ 5.1 Design & Introduction
- ▶ 5.2 Process Management:
       Product & Service
       Production & Delivery
- ▶ 5.3 Process Management:
       Support Services
- ▶ 5.4 Management of Supplier
       Performance

6.0 BUSINESS RESULTS
    6.1 Product & Service Quality Results
    6.2 Company Operational And Financial
    Results
- ▶ 6.3 Supplier Performance Results

7.0 CUSTOMER FOCUS & SATISFACTION
    7.1 Customer And Market Knowledge
- ▶ 7.2 Customer Relationship
    7.3 Customer Satisfaction Determination   Management
    7.4 Customer Satisfaction Results
    7.5 Customer Satisfaction Comparison

FIGURE 10.2

ISO 9000   ISO 9000 Unique

4.1 Management Responsibility
4.2 Quality System

4.16 Control Of Quality Records
4.20 Statistical Techniques

4.2 Quality System
4.4 Design Control
4.9 Process Control

4.3 Contract Review

4.18 Training

4.4 Design Control
4.5 Document And Data Control
4.6 Purchasing
4.9 Process Control
4.14 Corrective And Preventive
　　 Action
4.17 Internal Quality Audits
4.19 Servicing

4.8 Product Identification &
　　 Traceability
4.10 Inspection & Testing
4.11 Control of Inspection
4.12 Inspection & Test Status
4.13 Control of Nonconformity
　　　 Product
4.15 Handling, Storage, Packaging
　　　 Preservation and Delivery

4.7 Control Of Customer-
　　 Supplier Pruduct

4.3 Contract Review

FIGURE 10.2

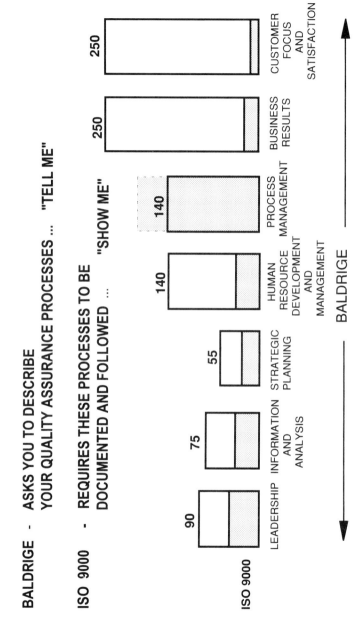

ISO 9000 VS BALDRIGE

BALDRIGE - ASKS YOU TO DESCRIBE
YOUR QUALITY ASSURANCE PROCESSES ... "TELL ME"

ISO 9000 - REQUIRES THESE PROCESSES TO BE
DOCUMENTED AND FOLLOWED ... "SHOW ME"

250 — CUSTOMER FOCUS AND SATISFACTION

250 — BUSINESS RESULTS

140 — PROCESS MANAGEMENT

140 — HUMAN RESOURCE DEVELOPMENT AND MANAGEMENT

55 — STRATEGIC PLANNING

75 — INFORMATION AND ANALYSIS

90 — LEADERSHIP

BALDRIGE

ISO 9000

FIGURE 10.3

134

COMPARISON OF BALDRIGE AND ISO 9000

	Baldrige	**ISO 9000**
1. Acceptance	U.S. (Only)	Worldwide
2. Application	Voluntary	Required (Worldwide)

3. Assessment	1. Self (As Needed)
	2. Recognition
	  A) Application Review
	  B) Site Visit
	  C) Feedback Report
		1. Self (As Needed)
		2. Registration
		  A) Quality Manual Review
		  B) Site Visit
		  C) Findings

4. Assessors	Independent Examiners Assigned by NIST Trained and Tested	Independent Examiners Hired by Client Accredited (ISO 9000)

5. Coverage	Total Quality Management System
	 • Comprehensive
	   Assessment of
	   Organization
	 • High Level Data
		Assurance of Processes
		
		 • Audit of Processes
		   Within Organization
		 • Detail Data

6. Criteria	Interpretive
	  7 Categories
	  24 Items
	  54 Areas
		Specification
		  20 Elements
		  46 Sub-Elements

FIGURE 10.4

135

COMPARISON OF BALDRIGE AND ISO 9000

	Baldrige	**ISO 9000**
7. Determination	• Assessment (Less Formal) • Numeric Score • Approach/Deployment /Results	• Assessment (Very Formal) • Pass/Fail • Process Documentation/ Controlled/Followed
8. Focus	• Continuous Improvement • Excellence • Prevention	• Conformance • Control • Correction
9. Followups	• Improvement Action Plan • Implementation	• Corrective Action Plan • Implementation
10. Frequency	• One Time (5 Years Re-apply)	• Initial Approval • Periodic Audits • Every 2-3 Years (Required)
11. Intent	• Stimulate & Motivate to New Levels of 1 Quality 2 Leadership	• Provide Customer Confidence in Supplier's Ability to Meet Contractual Obligations
12. Key	• Customer Satisfaction • Results	• Internal Operations • Responsibilities
13. Methodology	• Process Description	• Verification of Controls • Process Documentation

FIGURE 10.4

COMPARISON OF BALDRIGE AND ISO 9000

Baldrige	**ISO 9000**

	Baldrige	ISO 9000
14. Motivation	• Corporate Goal • Competition	• Contractual Conditions & Government Directives • Competition
15. Preparation	1. Understand Criteria 2. Develop Strategy 3. Collect Information 4. Prepare Application	1. Understand Standards 2. Develop Strategy 3. Prepare Documentation 4. Collect Evidence
16. Recognition	• Competitive U.S. Award • Use Award Logo	• Registration Certificate • Use Registrar's Mark

FIGURE 10.4

11 CONCLUSIONS AND SUMMARY

QUALITY is that elusive entity everyone is talking about. Customers want it! The media promotes it! Manufacturers, developers, providers, and suppliers seek it! Unfortunately, to paraphrase Francois Duc de La Rochefoucauld, "True (quality) [sic] is like ghosts, which everyone talks about and few have seen."

Although ISO 9000 is billed as an international quality standard, the fact remains that ISO 9000 says nothing about the eventual quality of the end product. So, how can ISO 9000 profess to influence a company's quality? One of the ways is by providing the foundation upon which to build. Remember, seeking an ISO 9000 certificate as the final goal is a mistake! It is only the beginning. ISO 9000 should be used as the means; one of a set of useful tools which can help you operate in a fashion that leads to ultimate customer satisfaction . This satisfaction in turn, provides for the realization of value (especially among your various shareholders)! (Figure 11.1)

Recognize that quality, itself, is a process. It needs a business purpose. Taken as an abstract will doom it to failure; as many other so-called popular quality movements (which caused an immediate furor in the business world and then burned out and eventually disappeared).

FIGURE 11.1

As newer business-oriented processes emerge, it's important to keep in mind that your overriding goal should be a focus on continuous improvement and the attainment of world class competitiveness. The concept of quality management (in any form) is a vehicle for building the necessary steps toward this fundamental goal. As is the case with ISO 9000, the staggering amount of resources, time, dedication, etc. will pay dividends in the future.

But how do you know when quality is good enough, or if you are on the right track? One of the basic measures of quality is embodied within the concept of "Customer Satisfaction." Fundamentally, if your customers are satisfied, albeit delighted or ecstatic, the chances are your quality is at the right level. Customers' perceptions regarding a company's quality play a large part in their overall impressions and certainly influence their satisfaction ratings.

As one embarks on an ISO 9000 program, it is a mistake to think that customer satisfaction is not one of the fundamental givens. Although ISO 9000 does not explicitly call out customer satisfaction as a major point, the underlying principles are inherent in the ISO 9000 program. When you seek ISO 9000 in order to "get the recognition" (certificate) which will enable your group, location, site, or organization to do business in the international arena, you are attempting to satisfy your customers. Even taking the time to document your procedures, maintain your records and harmonize the relationships of those around you is a form of customer satisfaction. But these are only a small part of the equation.

Customer satisfaction is more than being able to do business, and ISO 9000 can play a significant role. The Japanese business approach employs a concept which embellishes on the notion of customer satisfaction and is the art of "delighting one's customers" by doing what is unexpected — in a way that makes your customers eager to seek your goods or services. How then, can you approach this objective through ISO 9000? Do not go through the motions of merely describing your tasks or procedures (and ensure they're being followed), but use this opportunity to help anticipate your customers' needs (both within and outside your company). Strive to enhance these actions in a way that will continually delight your customers. Study the documented processes and say to yourself, "This is what I do, but am I merely satisfying those around me or is there something I could add (or change) which will allow me to go the extra step and perhaps 'happily' surprise those that receive my output (goods or services)."

The dictionary defines a customer as one who buys or does business, especially on a regular basis, and one with whom we deal regularly. It's interesting to note that most of us actually wear two hats—we are of course "suppliers" to our customers, but we are also "customers" ourselves (each time we receive goods or services in our business or in our personal lives). Working in the quality arena and having gone through an ISO 9000 program will result in the raising of everyone's quality expectations. We will no longer be satisfied with shoddy, inefficient work. We are no longer willing to adopt a laissez faire attitude or be willing to accept poor quality from those around us. There is a tendency to voice displeasure and, even worse to stop doing business with the people and functions who do not perform up to expectations. We see this in our business as well as personal lives. All in all, we are exhibiting the behaviors that our customers will exhibit! It is therefore incumbent upon each and every one to anticipate these actions and take the necessary steps to overcome any negative tendencies.

Companies that have already achieved ISO 9000 compliance have taken the FIRST STEP. Now is the time to build on these accomplishments. Do not be content with mere satisfaction, but "GO FOR THE DELIGHT."

In this context, ISO 9000 actually plays an extremely important role. By providing the ground rules for documentation and control, ISO 9000 establishes the baseline and facilitates the overall control. One of the best things about ISO 9000 is that it provides knowledge about the way things are done. And this knowledge is fundamental to improvement. Knowledge is the key—knowledge of how and why and when things are done. With it, one can work wonders; lacking knowledge condemns one to ignorance and waste.

One of the fundamental results of ISO 9000 is an established set of defined, documented and "adhered-to" procedures which reflect the current state of operations. Although often cited as being too bureaucratic, it is this relatively simple and straightforward result of the ISO 9000 process that will effectively lead toward new and improved ways to operate.

In a dynamic and ever-changing arena, an established set of well-defined, documented processes can lead to numerous internal benefits as well as provide assurance to your customers that a given business is serious about meeting their demands and requirements. A structured approach provides an additional benefit by creating a defined starting point for eventually measuring improvement and growth.

One of the main benefits of ISO 9000 is an improvement in the relationship between customers and their suppliers. While ISO 9000 appears to satisfy this objective, there is still some question as to the value of an external registration. Two of the obvious benefits of a third-party review and approval are: (1) external policing (2) advertising and dealing with the perceptions of the marketplace. The first may not be necessary if an organization has the full backing and support of the local management. When an organization implements ISO 9000 in the proper fashion, it is rare that an external assessor will uncover holes/gaps or other forms of nonconformances that the sponsoring group has not encountered. Remember, auditors do not "confer" findings as much as they "confirm" that which is already known. The second rationale dealing with marketing leverage or clout will diminish in value as the marketplace becomes more educated as to the actual worth of an ISO 9000 certificate.

Whether a third-party assessment is a measurable value or merely a perceived one requires insight into our customers' minds and expectations. There is little question that customers today require an ISO 9000 certificate as a condition of doing business. Recognizing this as the basic form of "doing what your customers want" and not as the final goal of our quality journey will allow us to properly place ISO 9000 within the framework of a total quality effort.

By itself, an ISO 9000 quality system is no more than its name implies, "a system." To be truly effective, the system must be part of an overall business strategy and approach. In order to fully appreciate the benefits of ISO 9000, there must be substantial, underlying reasons for establishing the quality system in the first place.

Perhaps the most vital aspect of the entire ISO 9000 program is the internal audit program, coupled with management's involvement in the status of the findings. Management can receive assurance that the work force is indeed following established, appropriate and highly-defined processes. Management can then turn its attention to dealing with various process-oriented issues, and one way to accomplish this is through the initiatives established by a TQM effort. The inter-relationship will result in improvements throughout the business.

As you pursue an ISO 9000 registration, many potential pitfalls and obstacles must be addressed and overcome. The essential key is SHARING! By utilizing the experience of the early ISO 9000 pioneers and learning from both their successes and failures, the result will be a methodology for demonstrating ISO 9000 compliance.

The ISO 9000 program will definitely prove to be a positive experience. Most of the benefits will accrue from the planning, preparation and internal audit programs employed throughout a company. Especially important will be the activities designed to resolve the identified nonconformances; and in most cases, leveraging these actions across numerous groups within your company. Finally, the external audits will help confirm your activities and findings.

There is little doubt that knowledge and understanding are the essential ingredients in a successful ISO 9000 venture. Early awareness and appreciation of the ISO 9000 standards, as well as deploying the learning and experiences throughout a corporation, are the keys to success. In the future, the challenge will be to integrate your ISO 9000 activities with your other quality system improvement methods and to make them transparent to everyday activities. You should expect to continue realizing benefits from your relationship with the external auditors by systematically identifying key problems and using the nonconformances as an impetus for improvement, not as an indication of "badness." Strive to make your business drive the quality system and seek to satisfy your customers and provide value to your shareholders.

Even though awareness of ISO 9000 is growing tremendously, the program continues to be under attack. It's too stringent. It's too narrow. It's too laborious. It's too bureaucratic. It's not TQM. It's too costly. It's too basic, etc., etc. However, only those who have lived through the entire process can really appreciate its impact and results! To borrow an often quoted precept "The value of a person's opinion on ISO 9000 is inversely proportional to the time since that person was directly involved in implementing and sustaining an ISO 9000 program." When one has taken the time to document the procedures (in a meaningful way), demonstrate that these procedures are being followed, been audited numerous times (by both internal as well as by external auditors), then, and only then, are they in a position to critique the program. It's like many other new concepts, it often gets criticized the most by those who have the least knowledge and experience.

To ensure that the ISO 9000 quality benefits continue to be realized, you will need persistence, persuasion, and above all, integrity of your convictions. You must believe!

———————— APPENDIXES ————————

APPENDIX 1. INTERNATIONAL ORGANIZATION FOR STANDARDIZATION

This organization, which is based in Geneva, Switzerland, is a worldwide federation of national standards bodies, one in each country. The object of the organization is to promote the development of standardization and related activities worldwide. The organization maintains a view toward facilitating the international exchange of goods and services and developing cooperation in the sphere of intellectual, scientific, technological and economic activity. The results of the organization's technical work are published as International Standards.

The scope of the activity covers standardization in all fields except electrical and electronic engineering standards, which are the responsibility of the International Electrotechnical Commission (IEC). The work of the International Organization for Standardization is carried out through the efforts of more than 2,700 technical bodies. Each year, over 20,000 experts from all parts of the world participate in the technical work, which has resulted in the publication of over 8,200 standards!

International standardization started in the electrotechnical field 80 years ago. While some attempts were made in the 1930's to develop international standards in other technical fields, it was not until the forming of the International Organization for Standardization in 1947 that a body devoted to international standards was created whose "...object would be to facilitate the international coordination and unification of industrial standards."

There are two types of representatives to the organization. Member Bodies are the national bodies "most representative of standardization" in their countries. These bodies are entitled to participate and exercise full voting rights on any technical committee as well as to become eligible for council membership and have seats in the General Assembly. At present, there are 76 Member Bodies. The United States representative (member body) is ANSI (American National Standards Institute).

The other type of membership is a Correspondent Member, which is generally an organization within a developing country that does not have its own national standards body. Correspondent members do not take an active part in the technical work, but are entitled to be kept fully informed about the work of interest to them. They may attend the General Assembly as observers. Nearly all the present correspondent members are governmental institutions. Currently, there are 20 correspondent members and 4 subscribers (those who only receive documentation).

The technical work is carried out through technical committees (TC). Each technical committee may, in turn, establish subcommittees (SC) and working groups (WG) to cover different aspects of work. At present, there are 182 technical committees, 630 subcommittees and over 1,900 working groups.

A proposal to begin work in a new field of technical activity normally comes from within the organization itself, but it may also originate from some other international organization. If accepted, the new work will be referred to the appropriate existing technical committee or a new technical committee will be established.

The end result of these activities is the creation of an international standard. Prior to becoming an international standard, a document must pass through a number of stages designed to ensure that the final result is acceptable to as many countries as possible.

When agreement is reached at the working committee level, the document is circulated as a Draft International Standard (DIS) for review and voting by all the members. If 75% of the votes are in favor of the DIS, it is accepted as an International Standard.

The majority of the work is done by correspondence, as each year over 10,000 documents are circulated.

Most of the standards require periodic revisions; often due to technological evolution, new methods and materials, new quality and safety requirements. To take all these factors into consideration, the general rule is that all standards should be reviewed at intervals of not more than five years. In fact, ISO 9000 recently went through a major revision cycle and the comparison of the 1987 version and the revisions (the "1994 version") can be found in Appendix 12.

APPENDIX 2. WORLDWIDE ACCEPTANCE OF ISO 9000 AS A NATIONAL STANDARD

Worldwide Acceptance:

Algeria	India	Slovenia
Argentina	Indonesia	South Africa
Armenia	Ireland	South Korea
Australia	Israel	Spain
Austria	Italy	Sri Lanka
Azerbaijan	Jamaica	Sweden
Barbados	Japan	Switzerland
Belarus	Kazakhstan	Syria
Belgium	Kyrgyzstan	Taiwan
Brazil	Malawi	Tajikstan
Bulgaria	Malysia	Tanzania
Canada	Mexico	Thailand
Chile	Moldova	Trinidad/Tobago
China	Mongolia	Tunisia
Colombia	Netherlands	Turkey
Croatia	New Zealand	Turkmenistan
Cuba	Norway	United Kingdom
Cyprus	Pakistan	Ukraine
Czech Republic	Papua New Guinea	Uruguay
Denmark	Peru	United States
Egypt	Philippines	Uzbekistan
Finland	Poland	Venezuela
France	Portugal	Vietnam
Germany	Romania	Yugoslavia
Greece	Russia	Zambia
Hungary	Singapore	Zimbabwe
Iceland	Slovakia	The European Union

APPENDIX 3. COUNTRIES' VERSIONS OF THE ISO 9000 STANDARDS

ISO 9000 has been adopted by numerous countries/governmental agencies as their national standard and has subsequently been translated into their own language. As the following chart indicates, some of these countries use their own nomenclature to refer to the ISO 9000 standards; for the most part they are identical:

ISO
ISO 9000	ISO 9001	ISO 9002	ISO 9003	ISO 9004

EC
EN 9000	EN 9001	EN 9002	EN 9003	EN 9004

AUSTRALIA
AS 3900	AS 3901	AS 3902	AS 3903	AS 3904

HUNGARY
MI 18990	MI 18991	MI 18992	MI 18993	MI 18994

INDIA
IS 14000	IS 14001	IS 14002	IS 14003	IS 14004

ISRAEL
SI 2000	SI 2001	SI 2002	SI 2003	SI 2004

JAPAN
JIS-Z9900	JIS-Z9901	JIS-Z9902	JIS-Z9903	JIS-Z9904

TANZANIA
TZS 500	TZS 501	TZS 502	TZS 503	TZS504

US
Q9000	Q9001	Q9002	Q9003	Q9004

ZIMBABWE
SAZ 300	SAZ 301	SAZ 302	SAZ 303	SAZ 304

APPENDIX 4. OBTAINING COPIES OF
THE ISO 9000 STANDARDS

1. The standards can be ordered directly from the International Organization for Standardization in Geneva:

    > ISO Central Secretariat
    > Case Postale 56
    > CH-1211 Geneva 20
    > Switzerland
    > (022) 741 01 11

2. The standards can be ordered directly from your country's representative to the International Organization for Standardization. For example, in the United States, the representative is ANSI (American National Standards Institute):

    > ANSI
    > 11 West 42nd Street
    > New York, New York 10036
    > (212) 642-4900

3. In some countries, professional societies or other related groups dealing with quality and/or standards also have the rights to distribute the ISO 9000 standards. In the United States, the American Society for Quality Control (ASQC) has the right to distribute the "American" version of ISO 9000:

    > ASQC
    > 611 East Wisconsin Avenue
    > Milwaukee, Wisconsin 53201
    > (800) 952-6587

APPENDIX 5. REGISTRARS OPERATING IN THE UNITED STATES

REGISTRAR	LOCATION/PHONE
ABS Quality Evaluations, Inc.	Houston, TX (713) 873-9400
AFAQ Inc.	Schaumburg, Il (708) 330-0606
A.G.A. Quality	Cleveland, OH (216) 524-4990
American Association for Laboratory Accreditation	Gaithersburg, MD (301) 670-1377
Amer. Euro. Services	Washington, DC (202) 337-3214
ASME	New York, NY (212) 705-8590
AT&T Quality Registrars	Union, NJ (800) 550-9001
American Quality Assessors	Columbia, SC (803) 779-8150
AV Qualite	Houston, TX (703) 465-2850
Bellcore	Piscataway, NJ (908) 699-3739
British Standards Institute	Vienna, VA (703) 760-7828
Bureau Veritas Quality International	Jamestown, NY (716) 484-9002
Davy Registrar Services	Pittsburgh, PA (412) 566-3086
Det Norskje Veritas	Houston, TX (713) 579-9003

DLS Quality Technology	Camillus, NY (315) 468-5811
Electronic Industries Quality Registry	Washington, DC (202) 457-4970
Entela, Inc.	Grand Rapids, MI (616) 247-0515
ETL	Cortland, NY (502) 476-9000
Factory Mutual Research Corp.	Norwood, MA (617) 255-4883
Global Registrars Inc.	Pittsburg, PA (412) 884-2290
Hartford Steam Boiler Inspection	Hartford, CT (203) 722-5294
Intertek Services Corp.	Fairfax, VA (703) 476- 9000
KEMA Registered Quality Inc.	Chalfont, PA (215) 822-4258
KPMG Quality Registrar	Short Hills, NJ (800) 716-5595
Lloyd's Registrar Quality Assurance Ltd.	Hoboken, NJ (201) 963-1111
MET Laboratories Inc.	Baltimore, MD (410) 354-3300
National Quality Assurance Ltd. Assurance	Boxborough, MA (508) 635-9256
National Standards Authority of Ireland	Merrimack, NH (603) 424-7070
NTS Registration Services	Acton, MA (508) 263-4811
OMNEX	Ann Arbor, MI (313) 480-9940

OTS Quality Registrars Inc.	Houston, TX (713) 688-9494
Perform Review Institute	Warrendale, PA (412) 772-1616
Perry Johnson Registrars	Southfield, MI (810) 358-3388
Quality Systems Registrars	Herndon, VA (703) 478-0241
Raytheon Quality Registrar	Burlington, MA (617) 238-2900
Scott Quality Systems Registrars	Wellesley, MA (617) 239-1110
SGS International Certification Services, Inc.	Rutherford, NJ (201) 935-1500
Smithers Quality Assessments Inc.	Akron, OH (216) 762-7441
SRI	Wexford, PA (412) 934-9000
TRA Certification	Elkhart, IND (219) 264-0745
TUV America	Danvers, MA (508) 777-7999
TUV Essen	Palo Alto, CA (415) 961-0521
TUV Rheinland	Newton, CT (203) 426-0888
Underwriters Laboratories Inc.	Melville, NY (516) 271-6200

(As of this printing, several other registrars have accreditation pending or may be planning to open offices in North America. Check with ASQC or ANSI for the most current information.)

APPENDIX 6. ISO 9000-3 GUIDELINE
FOR SOFTWARE AND TICKIT

The ISO 9000-3 document is divided into three parts: a quality framework, software life cycle activities, and supporting activities.

The framework is a very high-level description of the roles in quality to be performed by both the software supplier and the customer as well as a supplier-defined system for assuring quality throughout the software life cycle.

On the supplier side, ISO 9000-3 virtually mirrors the provisions of ISO 9001: in short, software developers should have formal, documented quality policies which are communicated and understood throughout the organization. Individuals should have the job responsibility and sufficient authority to implement such policies, and software suppliers should have specifically assigned staff and resources to conduct independent verification activities. Also recommended are a management representative to oversee the quality system and periodic management reviews to evaluate the effectiveness of the quality system.

Unlike ISO 9001, the software guidelines add a role for the customer in quality. ISO 9000-3 suggests that the customer appoint a management representative to deal with the supplier on contractual matters, including requirements definition, responding to questions, approving proposals, defining acceptance criteria and concluding agreements. Joint reviews between the buyer and seller of software deliverables are also suggested.

The quality system to which this framework refers is a basic component within each phase of the software life cycle. To make certain this is the case, ISO 9000-3 recommends that the quality system itself be documented, audits be taken to ensure that the plan is being carried out and corrective actions be undertaken as necessary.

Selection of the software development cycle processes and methods are left to the software developer. Like ISO standards generally, ISO 9000-3 activities are intended to apply to any software development process or method. For example, life cycle activities fall into nine general categories:

SOFTWARE LIFE CYCLE

1. Contact Reviews cover standard contractual items such as scope of work, contingencies and the protection of proprietary information;

2. Purchaser's Requirements Specification calls for a functional requirements specification, prepared by either a supplier or a customer and includes aspects such as performance, safety, reliability, security and privacy;

3. Mutual Cooperation pertains to issues like establishing requirements and managing the change control process;

4. Development Planning defines a development plan for moving from purchaser's requirements specifications to a software product. The Development Plan includes a project definition, organization of project resources, project phases, schedule, and references to related works like quality, configuration management, and test plans. Development Planning also cites the need for controlling inputs and outputs by phase and a method for monitoring and verifying progress;

5. Quality Planning calls for a separate, project-by-project quality plan;

6. Design and Implementation insists on a disciplined approach to software design, with early purchaser and supplier agreement on the amount of design-related information to be disclosed. The designer should use a systematic design methodology, utilize past experience, design with an eye towards maintenance tasks, and adhere to programming rules and conventions;

7. Testing and Validation notes the requirement for validation and testing at varying levels of abstraction. A test plan is suggested, covering such factors as level, test cases and data, environment and documentation. Testing itself should be appropriately recorded with problems affecting other parts of a system flagged and any program fixes retested. Validation of complete system and field testing are also addressed;

8. Acceptance covers the agreed-to terms and conditions governing the purchaser's acceptance of the delivered software product. Issues include acceptance testing, number of copies, medium used, delivery, and installation criteria;

9. Maintenance identifies maintenance as an issue in quality when this service is included in the purchase contract. Maintenance activities involve software changes and modifications, problem resolution, interface modifications, enhancements and upgrades. The standard addresses maintenance plans, documentation and release procedures.

Supporting activities represent the third major component of the ISO 9000-3 quality system. Such activities are not tied to a particular phase of software development. For instance, the standard cites the need for a configuration management system, including a plan, software item identification, traceability and change control. Document control covers issues such as types of documents to be produced, document reviews and approval and change management. Other categories listed as support activities include quality records, product and process measurement, tools and techniques and purchasing.

TICKIT

There is little question that the quality system involved in software development may be different from those used for other types of goods and services. One of the countries recognizing this has been the UK and, as a result of their investigations, the United Kingdom Department of Trade and Industry and the British Computer Society have created "TickIT," to interpret the ISO 9000-3 software development guidelines, expand the guidance this document provides developers, and serve as an accreditation body.

The TickIT scheme goes beyond the ISO 9000-3 guideline and attempts to use the guideline as a prescriptive standard. The TickIT program is divided into five sections, but only one of the sections deals with application of ISO 9000-3 to the ISO 9001 standard. The other sections include an introduction, an explanation of the customers' expectations, guidance for suppliers and guidance for auditors on the various methods to be used in conducting software audits.

All of the registrar's employees (assessors) have to conform to the performance standards outlined in the appendix of the TickIT document.

Currently, only the UK has adopted this scheme for registering software suppliers, and the number of registrars approved to perform software assessments under the TickIT scheme is limited. At this time, the other countries in the European Union (as well as the rest of the world) have not agreed to use the TickIT program for their software registrations.

The name "TICKIT" is a combination of two terms: in Britain, they use the term "tick" to denote what is referred to in the U.S. as a check mark. The "IT" at the end of the name, refers to information technology. In British parlance, the information technology is ticked (checked) upon approval, signifying acceptance. The TickIT symbol — consisting of a check mark, the letters IT and the European designation for the ISO 9001 standard (EN 29001) then becomes the company's "ticket" of admission to do business in the information technology field.

APPENDIX 7. ISO 9000 ACRONYMS

AENOR	Asociation Espanola de Normalization y Certificacion (Registrar)
ANSI	American National Standards Institute
ASQC	American Society for Quality Control
BSI	British Standards Institution (Registrar)
BVQI	Bureau Veritas Quality International - (Registrar)
CEN	European Committee for Standardization
CENELEC	European Committee for Electrotechnical Standardization
DANAC	National Accreditation Council of Denmark
DOD	U.S. Department of Defense
DNV	Det Norske Veritas (Registrar)
EC	European Community
EFTA	European Free Trade Association
EN 29000	European Norm (Quality standard series)
EOQ	European Organization for Quality
EOTC	European Organization for Testing and Certification
EQS	European Committee for Quality System Assessment and Certification
IEC	International Electrotechnical Commission
IST	Irish Systems and Technology (Irish Accreditation Council)
MOU	Memorandum of Understanding
NA	National Accreditation Council of Norway
NACCB	National Accreditation Council for Certification Bodies (UK)
NAC-QS	National Accreditation Council of Belgium
NCSCI	National Center for Standards and Certification Information

NA	National Accreditation Council of Norway
NIST	National Institute of Standards and Technology
NVCASE	National Voluntary Conformity Assessment System Evaluation
RAB	Registration Accreditation Board (U.S.)
RvC	Raad voor de Certificatie (Netherlands Accreditation Body)
SCC	National Standards Council of Canada
SINCERT	National Accreditation Council of Italy
SQS	National Accreditation Council of Switzerland
SWEDAC	National Accreditation Council of Sweden
TAG	Technical Advisory Group (In the U.S., it advises the U.S. TC #176)
TGA	National Accreditation Council of Germany
TC	Technical Committee (TC #176 is responsible for ISO 9000)
UNI-CEI	Italian Accreditation Body

APPENDIX 8. EUROPEAN COMMUNITY (EC) DIRECTIVES ON ISO 9000

There has been a great deal of misunderstanding and confusion regarding the European Directives which implied that ISO 9000 compliance was required to do business in Europe. Various questions have dealt with whether this is an enforceable law, will it really become effective, are there any special conditions, will the timing be all at once or will it be gradual (phased-in), does it apply across the board or only in special circumstances, etc.?

Clearly, the European Union (E.U.) has adopted ISO 9000 as their common quality system requirement and has, in fact, labelled it as "EN 9000." The European Union, on May 23, 1991, reported in the Official Journal of the European Communities, #91/263/EEC, that the member states should "...take the necessary measures" to ensure compliance with the council directive requiring ISO 9000 adherence with regard to a number of regulated industries. The actual date cited for compliance was to be "not later than 6 November 1992."

It turns out that this is NOT a law, but a directive which promotes the standardization of quality throughout all the members of the European community. However, given the acceptance of the directive, and the fact that a number of countries (including France, Germany, Italy and the UK) have already indicated that their intention is to make it a normal part of their federal procurements, it has obviously become an integral part of customers' requirements! Other countries will be following this direction, and there is every indication that this trend will cascade into the private sector as well.

Outside Europe, Canada is imposing ISO 9000 compliance for their federal PC procurement and Mexico, as a result of the NAFTA, is stating that ISO 9000 will be one of the indices of quality for moving products across the North American borders.

The result is that we seeing a growing acceptance of the ISO 9000 standard and with the acceptance, there will be an increase in the demand for suppliers to be in compliance. As is the case with a program of this size and impact, delays are inevitable as individual countries/customers get their acts together, but the feeling is that an across-the-board ISO 9000 requirement is imminent.

APPENDIX 9. UNITED STATES GOVERNMENT AND ISO 9000

The Department of Defense (DOD) and NASA have officially approved the use of ISO 9000 in their contracts. This will undoubtedly cause a surge among defense and aerospace contractors, as they will no longer have to maintain separate quality systems: one for commercial use and one for government contracts. Both the DOD and NASA will have the authority to require compliance with ISO 9000 and, in the case of NASA, the specific military quality policies will be phased out in deference to ISO 9000.

DOD and NASA will differ in terms of their acceptance of third-party registration. DOD will NOT require third-party registration nor (for the present) will the certificates be accepted in lieu of governmental audits. NASA will, however, give its purchasing offices the choice of accepting a third-party registration along with the proviso that it remains the responsibility of the procuring NASA safety, reliability, and quality assurance organization to assess the acceptability of their suppliers' quality management system.

NASA has been working with DOD to develop a joint handbook (DOD/NASA-HDBK-9000) for implementing the American National Standards Institute (ANSI)/American Society for Quality Control (ASQC) Q9000 standards. The expected benefits of these common DOD and NASA requirements approach will be realized from contractors who will not be required to maintain separate NASA and DOD quality management systems. This should translate into improved product quality, reduced costs, and enhanced international competitiveness.

APPENDIX 10. "CERTIFICATION" VERSUS "REGISTRATION"

There is a great deal of confusion and misinformation regarding the use of the terms "Certification" and "Registration" in regard to ISO 9000. It appears that these terms are NOT synonymous and one should be aware of the differences and legal implications.

According to the ISO/IEC GUIDE 2, 1991, Sixth Edition:

CERTIFICATION:

> Procedure by which a third party gives written assurance that a product, process or service conforms to specified requirements.

REGISTRATION:

> Procedure by which an authoritative body gives formal recognition that a body or person is competent to carry out specific tasks.

The definitions contained in this Appendix, as well as the definitions found in ISO Guide 48 (Guidelines for Third Party Assessment and Registration of a Supplier's Quality System), indicate that the intent for ISO 9000 is to register conformance (which implies an approach to provide information to the public about a supplier), rather than the more legalistic certification; which implies a form of warranty or guarantee. The international community appears to be maintaining the separation between registering a quality assessment and certifying products (e.g., environment, health and safety).

When a location goes through the ISO 9000 process successfully, it receives a registration that it complies with the relevant ISO 9000 standard. There is no warranty or guarantee of quality as implied by the use of the term certification.

The terms are often used interchangeably and perhaps, outside the United States, this is correct. However, in the U.S., it appears that ISO 9000 does not provide any legal warranty or guarantee of quality, therefore the preferred terminology is "registration."

APPENDIX 11. DETERMINING COMPETITION'S ISO 9000 STATUS

Unfortunately, there is no single, consolidated source of competitive ISO 9000 registrations! The present scheme relies on each and every individual registrar publishing its own list of registered sites/locations/companies. Since well over 170 registrars are doing business in the international environment (over 50 in the U.S. alone) it really isn't practical to poll these registrars for the information (most of the registrars will charge for their listings of the registered companies; including the updates which might be monthly, quarterly or annually). (See Appendix 5).

The International Organization for Standardization (contrary to what you might read in the press) does NOT maintain a list of registered organizations. Nor, for that matter does ANSI, ASQC, RAB or any of the other governmental or quasi-governmental agencies.

Many companies are in the pipeline and would not show up in a list of registered sites, since they are planning to be compliant at some future time. Since there are only 5,500+ registrations in the U.S. (66,000+ in Europe), it's probably of more interest to know what your competition is planning to do, as opposed to what they have already done. Occasionally, news items or press releases will refer to future plans, but again the information is incomplete. This leaves you with the problem of trying to understand what your industry is doing or thinking of doing. Perhaps the best way to address the problem is to contact your competitors directly! A simple call to the competitor's quality office will often produce results. In some cases, external organizations can contact the competitors, but generally speaking, it's probably best to go directly to them (in the same way one performs benchmarking).

Companies are often contacted by members of the press, independent consultants, students (writing term papers), competitors, and business partners—all asking about their ISO 9000 status (both accomplishments as well as future plans). I have no problem divulging this information (we are very proud of our accomplishments and are quite willing to share our successes and future quality directions with anyone!). Most companies are also proud of their ISO 9000 success (and potential successes) so they should be very willing to indicate their own ISO 9000 status.

APPENDIX 12. THE 1994 REVISIONS TO THE ISO 9000 STANDARDS

The emergence of Revision I (1994) represents the results of the International Organization for Standardization's actions to modify and improve the basic set of ISO 9000 publications. One of the ground rules of the organization is that all standards are subject to be revised after a five-year period (although in the case of the 1987 version, they have obviously missed their target). Part of the reason for the delay has been the unusually rapid acceptance of the standards and the fact that there are many more knowledgeable ISO 9000 experts involved in determining the scope and magnitude of the changes. In spite of the deliberations and compromises, the Revision I changes were approved at the September 1993 meeting of TC #176 in Budapest (the modifications were approved by a 90+% acceptance). Publication and general availability occurred in mid 1994.

Following is a summary of the changes found in **REVISION I**:

1. The changes represent almost a 50% rewrite of many of the ISO 9001 clauses (some alterations, some deletions, some additions, etc.) and the total size of the published documents has increased. For example, ISO 9001 has grown from seven pages to ten pages (43% increase).

2. ISO 9000 will be totally replaced by ISO 9000-1
   ISO 9004 will be totally replaced by ISO 9004-1
   ISO 9001:1987 will be totally replaced by ISO 9001:1994
   ISO 9002:1987 will be totally replaced by ISO 9002:1994
   ISO 9003:1987 will be totally replaced by ISO 9003:1994
   (The guideline documents, when updated, receive the
   "-1" notification. The auditable standards maintained their same numbering designation).

3. In the U.S. only:

The ANSI/ASQC versions are known as Q9000, Q9001, Q9002, Q9003 and Q9004 (instead of Q90, Q91, Q92, Q93 and Q94, which were the designations of the 1987 versions of the ISO 9000 standards).

4. One of the most significant aspects of the revision is the fact that the three standards will now have their respective clauses aligned. The number and content of the clauses in ISO 9001, ISO 9002 and ISO 9003 will all be the same. The idea is that all three differ only in the scope of coverage (i.e., the number of clauses that apply to a given business).

5. ISO 9001 continues to have the same 20 clauses as the 1987 version, but ISO 9002 will now have 19 of the 20 (the only missing one is Clause 4.4 Design Control).

6. ISO 9003 will have 16 of the 20 with the missing four being:

4.4	Design Control
4.6	Purchasing
4.9	Process Control
4.19	Servicing

7. Paragraphs throughout the standards have new documentation requirements. Some confusion existed in the 1987 versions as to when documentation was required and when it was not. The ISO 9001:1994 now shows that documentation is NOW REQUIRED in 16 of the 20 clauses including: responsibility and authority, quality systems, quality planning, contract review, design review, documentation and data control, purchasing, product identification and traceability, inspection and testing, control of measuring, inspection, test equipment, control of nonconforming product, quality records, internal quality audits, training and servicing.

8. The 1987 version of the standards did not have an explicit requirement for a quality manual. The 1994 version states that a quality manual is required and it should contain the documented procedures of a company's quality system.

9. There has been an attempt to eliminate the confusion over the terms "customer" and "purchaser." In the 1994 version, the term "customer" is used throughout (in place of "purchaser").

10. ISO 9001:1987 indicates that the standards are suitable for use in two-party contractual purposes. The 9001:1994 version states that the document is suitable for a supplier to demonstrate its capabilities as well as for an assessment of these capabilities by an external party (a registrar).

11. ISO 9001:1987 stated that requirements in the standard were aimed primarily at preventing nonconformances in all aspects from design to servicing. The 1994 version adds the notation that the requirements are aimed at achieving customer satisfaction by preventing these nonconformances.

12. New areas added:
    a) Stake holders & their expectations
    b) Industry Economic Sectors
    c) Quality factors (e.g., definition of needs, product design, conformance to design, product support, etc.)
    d) All work accompanied by process
    e) Recognized combination of four generic categories, e.g., Analytical Instruments

The implementation of the changes/additions will depend upon the individual registrar involved. The International Organization for Standardization does not consider these changes to be significant enough to manage the implementation on an international basis; therefore the final call will be left up to the individual registrars themselves.

Leaving open the decision of when to cut over to the revised standards raises some concerns regarding the voluntary nature of complying with the ISO 9000 standards. Imposing a specific time frame implies that an organization would not be afforded the opportunity to assess, for themselves and their customers, the value of the upgrade. The changes will involve additional resources, time, and ex-

FUTURE DEVELOPMENT

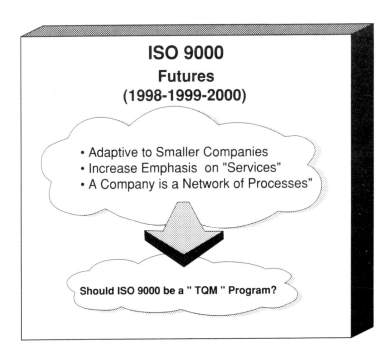

ISO 9000
Futures
(1998-1999-2000)

• Adaptive to Smaller Companies
• Increase Emphasis on "Services"
• A Company is a Network of Processes"

Should ISO 9000 be a " TQM " Program?

penses. In short, it would cease to be a voluntary migration. The action of dictating the specific timeframe, by the registrars, would make the cut over a de facto mandatory requirement.

ISO 9000 standard is voluntary, and all organizations should have the right to choose which nationally valid version of the standard they wish to self declare or be registered to by a third party. Unfortunately, due to the inaction of the various concerned parties, the time to move to the revised standards is being decided by the registrar organizations. For the moment, the practical concerns are outweighing the principles.

The transition period for registered companies will vary from three months to a year, although there is no set pattern. Most of the registrars appear to agree that they would be requiring audits for new customers to the revised standards soon after the standards are published, and the existing customers will probably be cut over during a scheduled surveillance audit.

APPENDIX 13.   ISO 9000 PUBLICATIONS

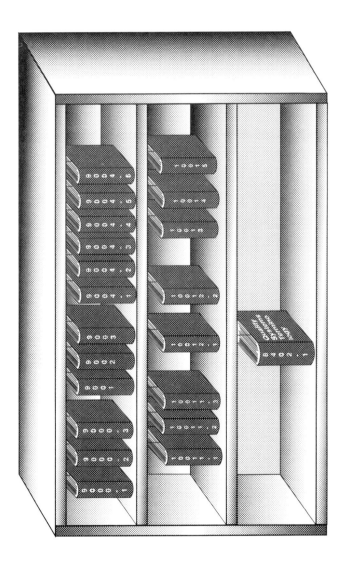

AUDITING
GUIDELINES

AUDITING
QUALIFICATIONS

MANAGEMENT
AUDIT PROGRAMS

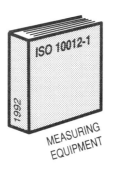

MEASURING
EQUIPMENT

MEASUREMENT
PROCESS CONTROL

DEVELOPING
QUALITY MANUALS

ECONOMIC EFFECTS
OF QUALITY

CONTINUING
EDUCATION AND
TRAINING

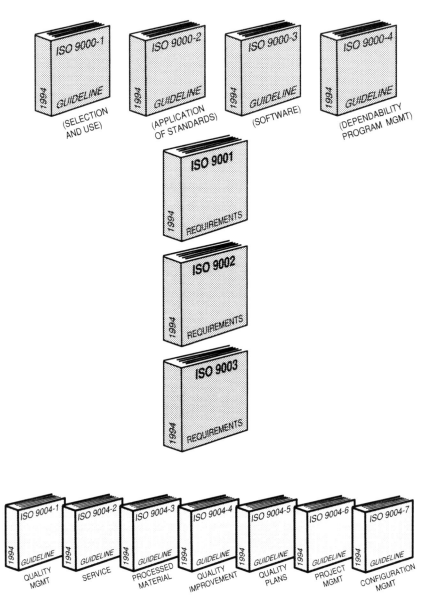

APPENDIX 14. ISO 9000 INFORMATION SHARING NETWORK

One of the best ways to keep everyone in your company on top of the ISO 9000 effort is through a consolidated and integrated information-sharing network. Clearly, use of this mechanism is optional, and it should be used as needed. Not all companies require every one of these facilities, and care should be exercised when selecting one or more for your own situation. The following is offered for your consideration:

1. A regularly published ISO 9000 newsletter containing:
   - a) the status of the various units
   - b) accomplishments
   - c) hints or useful tips
   - d) hindrances
   - e) a "where to find" directory
   - f) a "who to call" directory
   - g) any and all ISO 9000 -related information of interest to the community-at-large

2. "On-line" forums (e.g., interactive bulletin boards):
   - a) general information
   - b) comments
   - c) suggestions
   - d) questions
   - e) answers
   - f) implementation ideas
   - g) advice on tools and aids

3. A series of "Special Reports" covering items such as:
   a) registrar costs
   b) cost avoidance techniques
   c) confidentiality of information
   d) strategies for choosing between ISO 9001 and
      ISO 9002

Additionally, various organizations seeking registration have developed a number of tools which prove useful. Some examples of these include self-assessment questionnaires, a variety of documentation control programs, several library systems, and error correction and control systems. Additionally, many organizations have chosen to use an on-line system which acts as a single repository for all information required to comply with the ISO 9000 standards.

Generally, an on-line system contains the site's quality manual, department operating manuals, organization charts, linkages to various corporate and site operating procedures, a summary of the ISO 9000 standards, on-line/real-time data entry capabilities and hard copy (day-of-use) capabilities. Many different locations will incorporate department operations within the system, and these will identify (at an operating department level): the mission, strategy, goals, dependencies, deliverables, processes/procedures, management control system, change management, improvements, quality records, and update authorization. (See Chapter 7, "How to Implement an ISO 9000 Program").

One of the most beneficial approaches for sharing information is through the creation of an "ISO 9000 Data Base." An ISO 9000 data base can be established to provide a central, consolidated source for all pertinent ISO 9000 information. An example of this type of approach is found in Figure 14.1. Here, the data base consists of nine files with each highlighting a specific aspect of the program. Keep in mind that the information contained in these files must be as dynamic as possible in order to reflect the most current information available. The intention is to have the data readily available and easily accessible to anyone in the community. (Figure 14.2)

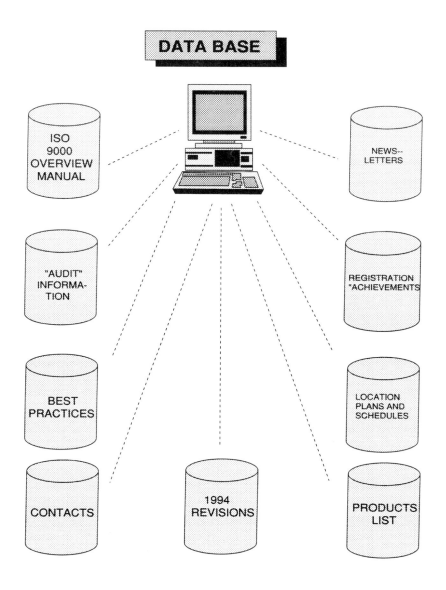

FIGURE 14.1

Following is a summary of the data base files:

THE ISO 9000 GUIDEBOOK

is an overview of the ISO 9000 program. It contains a history, a description of the standards, applications for their use, rationale for seeking registration, comparisons to your company's total quality management program as well as to the Malcolm Baldrige National Quality Award, and various other topics surrounding the ISO 9000 effort. It serves as a compendium of information and provides a source of data for both novices and experienced ISO 9000 practitioners.

THE ISO 9000 NEWSLETTERS

is a complete library of past ISO 9000 "Newsletters." The material deals with a variety of ISO 9000-related topics and assumes that the readers have obtained a basic understanding of the ISO 9000 program. Contained in the newsletters is useful information such as implementation hints, contacts, competitive status, current events in the international community and a shared repository of information gathered from many sources.

THE ISO 9000 AUDIT RESULTS

this document reflects the compilation of audit results from many of the organizations that were engaged in ISO 9000 assessment activities related to registration. It includes the size and location specifics of the various organizations, the level of ISO 9000 sought, a summary of all of the costs of the audits ($ and auditor-days), the discrepancies found (by both ISO 9000 element as well as by category, e.g., documentation, testing, calibration). There is also a section devoted to an

ISO 9000 INFORMATION REQUEST PROCESS

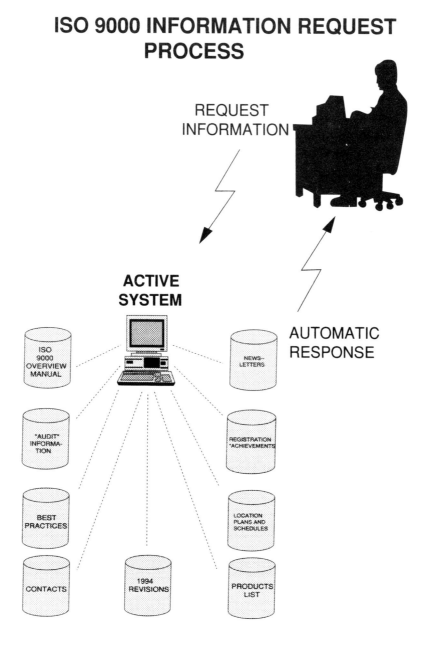

FIGURE 14.2

evaluation of the auditor's competence, ability to work with the location, relative satisfaction with the working arrangements, etc.

THE ISO 9000 BEST PRACTICES AND USEFUL TECHNIQUES GUIDE

is a compilation and repository of the various best practices which have been identified during the planning, implementation and review efforts of the various units seeking ISO 9000 registration. Although each location tends to have its own unique ways of solving issues, it will be extremely helpful to consolidate these best-of-breed practices in one place and allow readers to compare and contrast their own approaches. In many instances, these best practices often result in considerable savings in time and money.

THE ISO 9000 "PHONE BOOK"

is a listing of the ISO 9000 organizational contacts in the major elements of your business. In addition to the divisions and geographies, it should include contacts in the major distribution centers, subsidiaries and marketing offices. The individuals on this list agree to be contacted in order to provide information and insight relative to their own ISO 9000 efforts. It is a worldwide directory of ISO 9000 experts, each willing to share their experiences and assist others throughout the company, and will prove to be invaluable.

THE ISO 9000 IMPLEMENTATION SCHEDULES

this document reflects the current status of implementation plans and third-party registrations for all worldwide locations. In addition to identifying the organization, the plans indicate the level being sought, the date for a preliminary audit (if planned), the date the site is planning for its final audit, and the registrar being employed. It is a very useful tool for measuring the progress throughout the corporation as well as getting a current reading or pulse.

THE ISO 9000 "PRODUCTS" LIST

is a compilation of the products which are developed and/or manufactured by your laboratories and plants that have been registered to the ISO 9000 quality standards. As you know, the products themselves are not the subject of an ISO 9000 registration procedure; however, they are identified as being designed, developed and manufactured using the quality systems which have been registered in compliance. In many instances, customers will require a list of ISO 9000 compliant products (??) Since ISO 9000 only looks to a company's processes, you will either educate and correct the request by explaining the ISO 9000 philosophy or else provide a reverse listing which would answer the question. This file will allow you to choose the latter.

THE ISO 9000 REGISTRATION ACHIEVERS

is the summary listing of the worldwide organizations that have received formal ISO 9000 registration. It reflects the level of ISO 9000 (9001, 9002, or 9003), the name of the registrar, the division or business area and the name of the contact at the location who can provide additional information.

THE ISO 9000 REVISIONS

(Comparing the 1987 version to the 1994 version) is an educational document which takes each one of the 1994 revisions to the standards and highlights the change. It shows the additions, deletions and other alterations, while explaining the significance of the change as well as the potential impact to the existing quality system. This document will prove useful to your groups that might have already started on an ISO 9000 journey using the original standards. As the 1994 revision become more widely adopted, the need for this type of file will diminish.

APPENDIX 15. ADDITIONAL SOURCES
OF INFORMATION

U.S. Department of Commerce
National Institute of Standards and Technology (NIST), NIST has
information pamphlets on ISO 9000, quality system registration, and
related issues.
Publication Numbers: NISTR 4721 and NISTR 5122
National Technical Information Service
5285 Port Royal Road
Springfield, VA 22161
Tel: (703) 487-4650

Quality Systems Update
Monthly newsletter on ISO 9000 issues, lists of companies recently
registered, update on legislation, international reports.
Catalogue of all companies registerd to ISO 9000 in North America,
updated quarterly.
CEEM Information Services
P.O. Box 200,
Fairfax Station, VA 22039
Tel: (800) 745-556

Quality Progress
Magazine published monthly by the American Society for Quality
Control, is a peer-reviewed journal with articles on ISO 9000 and all
aspects of quality.
ASQC
P.O. Box 3005
Milwaukee
WI 5301-3005
Tel: (800) 527-8875

Quality Digest
Magazine published monthly by QCI International. Targeted at
management for quality, employee involvement, ISO 9000 and
related quality systems.
QCI International
1350 Red Bluff
CA 96080
Tel: (800) 527-8875

Quality
Magazine published monthly by Hitchcock Publishing Co.
Articles on quality, measurement, employee development for
engineering management and ISO 9000 quality systems.
Hichcock Publishing Co.
191 S. Gary Ave.
Carol Stream
IL 60188
Tel: (800) 633-4931

Information on the Malcolm Baldrige National Quality Award
American Society for Quality Control
P.O. Box 3005
Milwaukee, WI 53201-3005
Tel: (800) 248-1946

Information on the Shingo Prize for Excellence in Manufacturing
College of Business
Utah State University
Logan, UT 84322-3520
Tel: (801) 797-2279

Index